# forgive

## one another

# forgive

## one another

moving past the hurt
one step at a time

gloria chisholm

WaterBrook
PRESS

FORGIVE ONE ANOTHER
PUBLISHED BY WATERBROOK PRESS
5446 North Academy Boulevard, Suite 200
Colorado Springs, Colorado 80918
*A division of Random House, Inc.*

Some of the stories in this book are composites of several different situations; details and names have been changed to protect identities.

Scripture taken from the *Holy Bible, New International Version*®. NIV®. Copyright © 1973, 1978, 1984 by the International Bible Society. Used by permission of Zondervan Publishing House. All rights reserved.

ISBN 1-57856-311-9

Library of Congress Cataloging-in-Publication Data
Chisholm, Gloria, 1951–
       Forgive one another : moving past the hurt one step at a time / Gloria Chisholm.—1st ed.
       p.   cm.
    Includes bibliographical references.
    ISBN 1-57856-311-9
       1. Forgiveness—Religious aspects—Christianity.   I. Title.

BV4647.F55 C45  2000
234'.5—dc21
                                                                    00-035942

Printed in the United States of America
2000—First Edition

10  9  8  7  6  5  4  3  2  1

*To Merilee*

# contents

# acknowledgments

I want to thank my agents, Andrew Whelchel and Jason Cangia-losi, for their loyalty, support, constant encouragement, and, most of all, their belief in me as a writer and as a person.

I hardly know how to express my gratitude to my editor, Liz Heaney, who is also my friend. Wrestling together with many of the concepts of love and forgiveness has made both of us, I think, better people and has given us a deeper understanding of what it means to live in the world as authentic lovers and forgivers. She has helped me reach for the God-given wisdom inside of myself that I didn't even know was there.

Finally, I'm grateful to all of you "out there" who have taught me how to love and forgive. You've been so patient as I took bumbling baby steps, walking all over many of your toes in the process, while you acted as if you hardly noticed. Thank you.

# introduction

I don't remember when I first heard about forgiveness. Perhaps it was as a young Catholic when I learned that Jesus would forgive our sins if we asked him to. I took it very seriously, making the sacrament of confession a regular item on my Saturday to-do list. I would move into the confession booth, my flashlight and list of sins in hand. I didn't want to forget even one sin. I wanted to be clean.

As I grew into my teen years, still making sure I told the priest about every sin I committed and exactly how many times I committed it, my "punishment"—any number of Hail Marys and Our Fathers—seemed harsher. I was always up at the altar longer than anyone else was.

Was I a worse sinner or just more sensitive in confession? I'm not sure. In any case, that was the extent of my understanding of forgiveness. I've learned—and am continuing to learn—a lot about forgiveness. Especially since I made the choice to become a forgiver. I've learned that we can *desire* forgiveness, especially once we experience its benefits. We can also *resist* forgiveness. But we can't *understand* forgiveness—such grace doesn't make sense. Nor can we *demand* forgiveness of ourselves or of others. When we hurt someone, we can *hope* they will forgive us so that the relationship can be restored, but we can't force it.

I've also learned that though we can't manipulate forgiveness, we can work toward it. How? By admitting and feeling our pain while asking God to help us forgive. God offers us the gift of forgiveness. We need to open our hearts and receive it. But because we have been hurt so severely, we often don't activate forgiveness in our relationships. Instead, we close up to protect ourselves, and we can't receive the gift even when it's in front of our faces. This is true whether the gift is receiving forgiveness or offering forgiveness.

The key to a lifestyle of forgiveness, I've found, is first making the commitment to love our world. We can walk in forgiveness toward others and ourselves only if we've first committed to love. Unforgiveness blocks our ability to love; we will be motivated to be a forgiving person only if we've first decided to be a loving person.

As you read this book, do so with an open heart and a willingness to look at all your relationships. Is there someone you need to forgive? Is there someone who needs to forgive you? Forgiveness is not something God alone has the power to do, although he's probably the best at it. Because as Christians we have received God's forgiveness, we have access to his power to forgive those who have hurt us, no matter how deeply. Scripture tells us: "Therefore, as God's chosen people...bear with each other and forgive whatever grievances you may have against one another. Forgive as the Lord forgave you" (Colossians 3:12-13).

Forgiveness is one of the hallmarks of Christianity; we can forgive even when it doesn't make sense because it's not something that comes from within us. God has offered us this powerful gift, making it possible for us to offer it to others. This gift frees us to feel compassion and to act in love, even toward those who have harmed us. As well, when others forgive us, we are set free from the weight of their judgment and condemnation. Either way we win. Everyone wins. That is the power of forgiveness.

If you read a chapter a day of this book and follow the suggestions at the end of each chapter, you will have pondered and acted upon this power for twenty-one days—long enough, so I'm told, to form a habit. I suggest you make the following commitment before you go any further:

> *I commit to forgive—deeply and from my heart—any and all who offend me, every day, every hour, every minute.*

If you can honestly do this, you'll have the opportunity at the end of this book to turn your commitment into a lifetime vow.

*Chapter One*

# empowering
# yourself

"You hate him, don't you?" The counselor across from me dared me to answer him directly.

"What?" I said, shocked. "Hate him? Of course I don't hate him. I'm a Christian."

"What does that have to do with it? You still hate him."

"That's not true," I said quickly. "Hate the sin, not the sinner..."

The counselor rolled his eyes, then nodded. "You hate him. You might as well say it."

Now I was getting mad. "Why should I say it if...if..."

"Look at how he physically and emotionally abused you, how his abuse damaged your faith, how he neglected your kids—"

"I know, I know..." I just wanted him to stop.

"What about that time he offered you twenty bucks for sex? That time he raged at you for crying over your grandmother's death? That time he made you go out and wash the car the day after you'd had a baby? All those times he hit you—"

"Okay, okay, maybe I hate him. I don't know," I said, confused.

"You have every reason to hate him. He was mean, cruel—"

"Yes, it's true. He was. I do. I hate him. You're right—"

"How much do you hate him?"

"I hate him with everything, with all my…" Suddenly I was sobbing. "I hate him! I hate him! I hate him!"

This moment was a turning point in the process of forgiving my ex-husband for thirteen years of abuse and cruelty. The counselor, in all his wisdom, knew that until I admitted the hatred in my heart, I couldn't move forward in forgiveness and ultimately, love. I sat sobbing for many long minutes. Then, as my sobs subsided, the counselor said quietly, "Now what's under that hatred?"

I stared at him blankly.

"What do you feel now for your ex-husband?"

I couldn't believe it. It was as if God had waved a magic wand over my head. "Love. I feel love."

Later I might have dismissed the love I'd felt as a contrived and manipulated emotional reaction to the session with my counselor, but the next time I saw my ex-husband, my response told me something drastic had taken place. I felt genuine love and compassion for him. I had not felt that way about him for years. I even spontaneously reached out to touch his arm at one point, something I would never have done before. I hadn't been able to stand the sight of him, let alone ever imagine touching him again.

I began to understand that day that for those of us who have made the overall decision to love our world, God's empowering kind of love always lies beneath our anger and hurt. The secret was to learn how to tap into this power, to begin to understand and practically apply all I'd ever learned about love and forgiveness. Up until then, I think they may have been just words I casually threw around in the context of discussions about my Christian faith. Nice, warm words—*love* and *forgiveness*—but did I really know what they meant?

The idea was kind of scary. I knew I had a lot of internal work to do if I was going to live in the world as a loving, forgiving person rather than as a bitter and cynical one. There was the "church," with whom I'd had a big problem for many years. Oh, and my daughter, who was out of control for longer than I care to think about…and my mother, who couldn't give me the love and nurturing that I needed…and that friend who had betrayed me…and back to my ex-husband, who had continued to do things over the years that I continued to have to forgive.

I certainly had every reason to be bitter and hateful. We all do. If you're reading this book, you have likely been hurt and are finding forgiveness difficult—or seemingly impossible. You're not alone. We've all been hurt, abused, treated unkindly, betrayed, violated, ignored, victimized… Who wouldn't be a bit hardened after suffering so many injustices—often at the hands of those we love and who claim to love us? In fact, the people we care about *are* the ones who hurt us most. That's why the pain penetrates so deeply. If we didn't care we wouldn't hurt as much, if at all.

(By the way, we can't talk about love and forgiveness without mentioning that there are all kinds of folks in the world who are possibly in therapy right now because of what *we've* done to *them*… Just thought I'd mention that.)

Anyway, as we think about forgiveness and how it works—or doesn't work—I think we can all agree that it's not often an overnight event. We forgive a little bit, then a few days or even years go by, and we forgive a bit more. It's a process, and the first step in the process is to empower ourselves.

I believe we empower ourselves through the overall decision to love our world. If we can make that decision, we can make any decision God calls us to make. Love fuels all our decisions about how we treat the people in our lives. I didn't just make this up; it's a scriptural principle. "Therefore, as God's chosen people, holy and dearly loved, clothe yourselves with compassion, kindness, humility, gentleness and patience. Bear with each other and forgive whatever grievances you may have against one another. *Forgive as the Lord forgave you. And over all these virtues put on love,* which binds them all together in perfect unity" (Colossians 3:12-14, italics mine).

Forgiveness is simply one more way we can love our world. Granted, forgiveness can be difficult to get to because, to access it, we have to uncover a lot of pain. But once we've decided to be expressions of God's love in the world, we can't *not* forgive. A refusal to forgive would violate our own decision, go against our own value system, the one we've consciously chosen.

The truth is, the act of forgiveness empowers us in and of itself. When we are walking in an attitude of love and forgiveness, we are full of power, able to conquer anything that comes our way. Contrary to popular opinion, true power is not an external serendipity that comes with a particular position in a job or relationship. No, we attain true power when we know down to our toenails that we can face, with grace and dignity, whatever comes our way.

## Ask Yourself

Have I made the decision to love my world? What, if anything, may be hindering me?

Do I feel empowered to forgive anyone for anything, no matter how grievous the offense? Why or why not?

Is there anyone right now that I know I need to forgive? Who?

What am I willing to do to empower myself?

## To Do

Make a list of everyone who has ever hurt you. Include the grocery clerk who was rude to you, the cop who unjustly gave you a ticket, the kid who always rides his bike through your yard, as well as your parents, spouse, kids, boss, coworkers, and friends. Now, put a check by each person you know you haven't forgiven or aren't certain you've forgiven. (This exercise will only be helpful if you're 100 percent honest.) These are the relationships or incidents we will focus on during the next few weeks of the forgiveness process. Finally, if you can make the decision to love your world, decide also that you will do whatever is necessary to forgive each of these people. Commit to forgive.

*Chapter Two*

# it's more than one, two, three

Forgiveness is a process, as is love, honesty, loyalty, commitment, and just about anything else God requires of us. Sadly, some people in the Christian community put pressure on each other to forgive NOW, implying that if we can't forgive NOW, we are out of God's will or in sin or unrepentant.

I met Jessica around the time she was first acknowledging how angry she was at her mother. Jessica grew up feeling like her mom neither liked nor accepted her. She denied her anger for years, even though the signs were evident all along: Her mother constantly irritated her, and it was all Jessica could do to be civil to her, let alone patient or kind.

When it became too exhausting to suppress her anger any longer, Jessica let down her self-protective defenses and got in touch with her rage. Her pain was so deep that she couldn't even stand to be in the same room with her mother. The intensity of her anger frightened her. Not knowing what else to do, she told her mom that she wasn't going to be able to see her for a while, that she was angry and needed some distance if they were ever going to have a more loving relationship. Jessica wanted to forgive her mother, but she knew it would take time.

Jessica's mother was deeply hurt and didn't approve of Jessica's decision. "Why won't you forgive me?" she demanded. "How can you call yourself a Christian and not be willing to forgive me?"

"Mom, I want to forgive you, but I can't right now, and I'm not going to tell you I've forgiven you until I know that I truly have. I'm not saying I won't forgive you; I'm saying I can't right now—but I'm working on it." Even though Jessica didn't give in to her mom's manipulative pleas, she sometimes wondered if she was doing the right thing.

Fortunately for Jessica, she had many wise friends and a Christian counselor who assured her that forgiveness was a process and that she wasn't being rebellious or sinful by admitting that she wasn't ready to forgive her mother.

Have you ever felt rushed to forgive an offender, maybe by a member of your family or because of a sermon you've heard at church? You feel guilty because you still feel angry or hostile toward that person, and you may think God is displeased with you. So once again you say the words "I forgive you" to yourself or even to the person. Still, just thinking about him or her causes your anger to resurface. Each act of forgiveness has its own timetable; it can't be rushed or forced by you or by anyone else who thinks you should be in a different place than you are.

The apostle Paul told the Ephesians to "be kind and compassionate to one another, forgiving each other, just as in Christ God forgave you" (Ephesians 4:32). He used the word *forgiving* rather than *forgive*, which suggests an ongoing process or lifestyle of forgiveness. This implies that forgiveness is something we offer on an ongoing basis. Too often we do a terrible disservice to those from whom we demand forgiveness, not giving them the time they need to work through the feelings, grieve the losses, and *choose* to let go of their pain. Forgiveness takes time. Period.

How much time it takes varies from individual to individual, depending on the depth of the wound and the personality of the wounded as well as how the offender responds and continues to respond. The forgiveness process can often be speeded up when there is true validation of the offense, then repentance and sorrow on the part of the offender.

That was true for Jessica, who remained true to her feelings and her desire to move toward forgiveness. In time her mother began to realize that whether she had intended to or not, she clearly had wounded her daughter. She wrote Jessica the following letter:

> I don't excuse myself or blame anyone else for my
> attitudes and actions toward you.... When you told
> me over two years ago of your feelings, I began to
> have an idea of your struggles. That pained me
> because I realized that I must have broken your
> spirit. I am asking for your forgiveness for my failure
> to express my love, for my contentious spirit, and
> for the subsequent breaking of your spirit.

Jessica says that this validating letter lifted a weight off her shoulders and helped her move more quickly toward forgiveness. Her mother had taken personal responsibility for her behavior and had acknowledged the pain she had caused.

The amount of time it takes to be able to forgive an offense is relatively unimportant, especially to God. He wants us to move through the process soulfully, listening to him at every step. What's critical is not how slowly or quickly we move but that we keep our hearts open. What matters ultimately is who we become as a result of feeling our pain and choosing to forgive, thereby choosing to love our world. Yes, God wants us to forgive…but that can't happen unless we are becoming more like him and cooperating in the process.

How do we cooperate with God in the process of forgiveness? How do we know when he wants to do something in us? We listen to him and to our feelings. Jessica entered therapy in order to grieve her relationship with her mother. Because she had denied her feelings for so long, she needed to experience the pain and isolation she felt.

She would see a mother and daughter laughing in the mall and know she needed to forgive her mom for all the moments they'd missed together because her mother was busy or emotionally unavailable.

She would watch a movie in which a mother and daughter exchanged the words "I love you" and know she needed to forgive her mother for her inability to say those words.

The day came, however, when Jessica suddenly realized that she *had* forgiven her mother. Her mom called one day, unexpectedly, and for the first time in years Jessica didn't respond in irritation or anger. She treated her mother just like she would have treated anyone else. God had worked mysteriously in her heart, and when she was ready he gave her the ability to forgive. The process took about five years.

Just this last year Jessica's mother gave Jessica an unanticipated gift with these words: "I've been meaning to tell you something. I feel really good about our relationship now—I feel like we've resolved all the issues between us, and I'm very happy about that. I don't know if that would have happened had you not come to me fifteen years ago and told me how angry you were. I didn't like it at the time and was hurt and angry with you…but it forced me to look at myself and take some responsibility for my actions. As a result I changed and also took action to make amends with other members of the family. I wanted to thank you for what you did and let you know that I think you did the right thing."

Of course, going through the forgiveness process can't guarantee that a broken relationship will be restored or that the other person will change or validate your pain. In a broken world, that doesn't always happen. But entering the forgiveness process puts us in a place where such things are possible.

Don't be afraid to enter into the process. At the end you will find a prize—a depth of unimaginable love for the one who hurt you. For one golden and soulful moment you have transcended your humanness to achieve a divine position of love just like the one Jesus modeled for us on the cross.

At the end of the process, what you'll find is compassion.

*Ask Yourself*

Whom have I avoided forgiving because it would be too painful to enter the process?

If I could have a heart-to-heart conversation with that person or those persons, what would I say?

What one step can I take today toward forgiveness of that person or group of people?

*To Do*

Write a letter to someone who has hurt you. Let it be as long as it needs to be. Talk about how the pain felt, how deeply it penetrated, and why. Validate your own feelings. You didn't deserve this pain. Now it's up to you to decide whether or not you will grieve the pain and work through your feelings so you can choose to love your world—all of it. Whether or not you choose to mail your letter is also up to you.

# Chapter Three

# cooperating with the process

Healing and change rarely take place overnight. As we've seen, forgiveness takes time. And unfortunately, the process feels uncomfortable. We don't know what to do. We'd much prefer a quick fix or five clear steps to health and wholeness.

We don't know why, but God chooses to use a process. He didn't even create the world in one moment; creation was a six-day process. Where did we get the idea that things need to be done in a hurry—especially something as important and significant as forgiveness?

When we're in the forgiveness process, something feels incomplete. It *is* incomplete. Scripture tells us we can be *confident* "that he who began a good work in you will carry it on to completion until the day of Christ Jesus" (Philippians 1:6). Paul is referring here to God's assurance that he is constantly shaping and molding us, making us more like him. Spiritual transformation is a process, one that will continue throughout our lives.

Forgiveness is a big job, and we need to take the time to do it right. One reason we're so messed up as adults is because as little kids we were never given the opportunity to process our hurts so that our wounds could heal. Too often someone would hurt us—our parents, siblings, or peers—and we were not allowed to cry or get angry or express our fear.

We might have heard, when we were hurt: "Now don't you cry, or I'll give you something to cry about…" The message was that being hurt in and of itself was not a reason to cry.

When we were angry: "If you can't say something nice, don't say anything at all." In other words, "It's not okay to express your anger."

When afraid: "No, you're not afraid, there's nothing to be afraid of…" The point was that we couldn't trust our feelings because we didn't really feel what we thought we felt.

I once heard author and speaker John Bradshaw talk about a time when he was eight years old and upstairs alone in his room while his parents were having a party downstairs. Scared, he came downstairs and announced, "I'm afraid."

His parents and the other adults immediately corrected him. "No you're not. There's nothing to be afraid of."

He was puzzled. *I was sure I was afraid,* he thought as, invalidated, he went back upstairs denying his real feelings.

I have a friend whose mother died when my friend was eight years old. A short time later her father married his deceased wife's sister.

"I want you to call her 'Mom,'" he instructed his young daughter.

But she couldn't. Her mom was dead. She missed her. She hadn't even had a chance to grieve her mother's death before her father married again.

"Daddy, I can't—"

"Yes you can. And you will."

My friend was not allowed to process her pain, to heal. She needed time to grieve and then to adjust to having a new "mother" around. She should have been given the right to choose whether or not to call this woman "Mom." The choice would have honored her process. When we're not given a chance to heal from one wound before another is inflicted, we begin to lose touch with our feelings. We become focused on protecting ourselves from the current blows, which prevents us from healing past wounds.

If it's true that "[God makes] everything beautiful in its time" (Ecclesiastes 3:11), then we need to make sure that we're providing a space for God to work in our own lives and in the lives of others. We need time: time to grieve losses, time to feel our feelings, time to heal, time to forgive, time to bring the offense to a resolution with the offender.

But what if it takes many months, maybe even many years, to forgive someone else? What if the offender dies before we can resolve the offense?

Good questions. It may comfort you to know that God is not concerned that you become perfect, only that you stay committed to his process of perfecting you—that you keep maturing, spiritually and emotionally. The Greek word Jesus used when he instructed us to be "perfect" (Matthew 5:48) can be translated as "ripe" or "mature." God is the one who provides and orchestrates opportunities for the forgiveness process, but you are the one who says yes or no to those opportunities. If you miss one opportunity, you can bet God will come around again with another.

One day our office staff was having a meeting, and I was saving a seat for a friend. Another friend approached. As she began to sit down next to me, she asked, "Is this seat taken?"

"It is—" I began, but she was already bolting from the room in tears.

Later, when we talked, she confessed that this seemingly small incident had connected her to feelings of rejection from a significant person in her childhood. She obviously hadn't yet completed the process of forgiveness with this individual. I knew this wasn't the first and wouldn't be the last opportunity God would provide for her to keep moving through the forgiveness process.

Every person's process is different, of course, but for my friend to move ahead in forgiveness, I believe she needed to: (1) feel her feelings and not "bolt" from them—even though she may have needed to bolt from the room; (2) try to understand what was behind those feelings. Then, once she understood the source of her reaction, she needed to: (3) try to understand where the original offender was coming from; (4) receive compassion from God and offer it to the offender; and (5) ultimately extend forgiveness (which usually means committing once again to the process, as long as it takes). These steps rarely happen all at once, but forgiveness usually doesn't occur until we go through each of these stages in the process.

Do you always recognize when God presents you with an opportunity to grow in forgiveness? I don't. Sometimes I suspect it might be an opportunity, and I ignore it. "Oh yeah, well, I do have some feelings about what just happened, and I'd just love to work on forgiving (I could insert any of a number of names here), but I'm a little busy. Maybe later."

It's not that I don't want to work on forgiveness. It's more that the opportunity comes to me in the form of an uncomfortable feeling in my gut, one I can't identify—and one I can easily repress with a brownie or something. I know unconsciously that if I stop and identify what I'm sensing, I'm going to feel some very uncomfortable feelings. Who wants to sign up for that in the middle of one's busy day?

Forgiveness requires hard work. Who wouldn't rather be surfing the net or playing golf than sitting around feeling the pain of an injustice in order to move through it to forgiveness? We put off engaging in the process until Monday, but Monday comes and we're tired from working all day—and besides, we don't have any particularly angry or hurt feelings or anything right now, so we think we must have forgiven so-and-so. We forget about our anger and hurt until so-and-so comes around and Boom! We're hit once again with all of this rage, or we suffer a crying streak and wonder what's going on.

When we avoid the process and repress our feelings, we usually don't treat other people well.

"What's wrong? Is anything wrong?"

"No," we snap. "What makes you think anything's wrong?"

"Oh, I just kind of thought—are you sure nothing's wrong?"

"Look, nothing's wrong," we say, but our voice has a distinct edge to it. "If something was wrong, I'd tell you."

"You seem a little, uh, on edge or something."

We continue to repress, or if we're pushed far enough, we'll growl and snap some more, never dealing directly with whatever the person did to hurt us or make us angry. Of course, we're lying when we say nothing's wrong. What would be more honest to say is, "Yes, something's wrong, but I don't feel safe enough to talk about it."

If we want to live in forgiveness, we need to watch and be alert to the opportunities God gives us to grow in forgiveness. When God gives us these opportunities, we can answer yes or we can answer no. We can't say "maybe later." Waiting isn't an option because to say "wait" is to say "no." If we don't enter into those opportunities God gives us, we're saying "no" to spiritual growth.

But God doesn't ask us to do anything we aren't equipped to do. He's always patient with us. When we ask him, he works in our hearts so that we are able to forgive, over time, even the deepest hurts.

We can trust God with our hearts.

## Ask Yourself

Am I repressing my angry and/or hurt feelings? What are they?

Am I ignoring any opportunities that God may be providing me to learn more about the forgiveness process? Can I identify one or two of these?

Am I listening too much to those around me who think I'm not moving fast enough? What am I hearing? How can I get the strength I need to turn off those voices and listen to God's and my own?

Am I allowing myself the time it takes to forgive those who offend me? How can I go about being more compassionate with myself in the process?

Am I happy with my progress? What would it take to make me feel satisfied with my forgiveness process?

## To Do

Spend a few minutes today thinking about any unfinished business you need to address. Sit with the feelings that come up as you think about the people and situations that have offended you. Where are you in the forgiveness process? Are you moving or are you stuck? If you're stuck, take a step to get unstuck. The best way to do this is to find a way to access the feelings that were wounded. Have a friend ask you some questions to unlock your emotions. After expressing the feelings, see if you can find any compassion to forgive. If you can't, that's okay. Commit to try it again at another time.

*Chapter Four*

# choosing your
# process

I smiled when I saw Jerry approaching me after the conference workshop.

"Are you enjoying the conference?" I asked.

"Yes, but you know that letter you helped me with?"

I nodded.

"Well, guess what, it hasn't helped me."

I had given Jerry my professional advice about how to write a query letter that would grab a literary agent's attention at this writing conference.

"The last agent I talked to agreed to look at my novel, saying the reason he turned me down the first time was because I'd left the most important stuff out of the query letter. And with two other agents, it was already too late. After reading my query letter, they didn't want to talk to me at all." He paused.

I think I was in shock.

"How long ago was our consultation?" he asked.

"About six weeks."

"Did I pay you by check or cash?"

"I don't remember," I said, shaking my head. "Excuse me." And I walked away to extricate myself from the conversation.

What had just happened? I tried to clear my head, realizing that Jerry had just blamed me for his failure to secure a literary agent's interest in representing him. Then I remembered another time, not long ago, when Jerry had criticized a seminar I'd put on for writers. "I'm never going back to that," he'd said huffily. "A bunch of touchy-feely women who just want to talk about the touchy-feely writing process instead of really getting down to writing."

He'd later e-mailed me an apology for his judgmental attitude, but by then I'd realized he was a judgmental, critical person. Bottom line, I needed to forgive him—and then consider not interacting with him again because of his abusive push-pull way of relating.

Did I have that choice? Could I choose what my forgiveness process would look like? Does forgiving someone mean I have to continue interacting with that person? Am I obligated to give a second chance to someone who has hurt me? Sometimes, but maybe not always.

Peter asked Jesus, "'Lord, how many times shall I forgive my brother when he sins against me? Up to seven times?' Jesus answered, 'I tell you, not seven times, but seventy-seven times'" (Matthew 18:21-22). What did Jesus mean? Did I literally have to give Jerry seventy-five more times to be rude before I stopped interacting with him? I don't think so. Jesus isn't talking here about how we are to *interact with* our offenders. All he says is that we need to forgive—a lot. Over and over and over again.

God lets us choose what forgiveness means in the context of each individual relationship. He knows our hearts and whether or not a relationship would be a good thing for us to pursue. We may choose to forgive someone and then relate on a limited basis to that person in the future. Or, depending on how hurtful the offense, we may choose to forgive, let go, and go on as if nothing had happened. Or we may choose to end our relationship with that person.

In my case, I was able to forgive Jerry quickly because the hurt I experienced was not deep. Forgiving him simply meant (1) letting him slip out of my life without going around telling everyone how rotten he was and (2) feeling neutral rather than hostile every time his name came up among our mutual friends.

When you or I have been hurt by someone, we are not victims, powerless to protect ourselves from repeated offenses. We have choices. We get to decide what we can and cannot do when it comes to our relationship with an offender. If we are consistently being violated in a relationship, and the other person is not respecting our boundaries, then we have another choice. Do we want to back away physically and emotionally while forgiving the offender in our heart? Or will we continue to set ourselves up for more violation? This is true whether the offender is a family member, friend, or colleague.

How do we decide what our future relationship with this person will be? What do we need to look at as we establish our boundaries? One important element is our level of commitment to the relationship before the offense took place. Jerry was a professional acquaintance, not a longtime friend, so I felt no commitment to

him like I would to a husband or child or close friend. Consequently, I chose to cease interacting with him.

Of course, with my children I will go mile after mile after mile,
as they've proved they will with me. The forgiveness process must
continue so that no one—neither the offended nor the offender—
is left in the prison of bitterness, resentment, and unforgiveness.
That's not to say there aren't times when even parents and children
must part ways. Sometimes, even in families, the offenses are so
grievous that all attempts to interact only do more damage—akin
to throwing oneself off a cliff or under the wheels of a locomotive.
Why do that to yourself unless you have a death wish?

If you don't trust yourself to do the loving thing in the forgiveness process, that's okay. You can trust God to guide you in your
personal relationships and in choosing how to move through the
forgiveness process. He will always, if consulted, let us know the
condition of our hearts. And once we're aware of what to work
on—our selfish motives, self-protective strategies, hostile attitudes—he will always give us the choice as to how to proceed in
our relationships with others.

When anyone starts to advise you as to how you should go
about forgiving, ask God for discernment and check in immediately with your own heart. Trust what you find there—do you even
*want* to be in any kind of relationship with the offender?

The process of forgiveness is an individual one. Who knows us
best? God created us, and he knows we don't respond well to pressure from others to change or to do anything that is not yet in
our hearts to do. He is the one who puts the desire to change
and/or grow in our hearts. Trust what you sense he is leading you
to do.

*Ask Yourself*

Am I feeling the pressure from anyone outside myself to forgive another person in a way that allows him or her to continue to treat me in an unloving way?

How can I take care of myself and still forgive?

What is God requiring of me in the relationships where forgiveness seems to be what I'm supposed to be learning?

*To Do*

Consider the person in your life you're having the most difficulty forgiving. If you could change the pattern of relating to that person in the future, what would you change? Take a step today toward making that change.

*Chapter Five*

# positioning
# your heart

When was the last time you woke up in the morning and asked God to help you forgive those you needed to forgive? To help you recognize the opportunities to forgive that might come your way that day?

What is the first thing that comes to mind when someone runs into your brand-new SUV? Or a family member washes the clothes and your favorite T-shirt turns pink because he or she put the colors and the whites together? On a more serious note, what do you do when a close friend says something mean about you behind your back? Or your daughter has an abortion and only tells you after the fact? Or your boss fires you?

Is your heart positioned in such a way that you know instantly what your role is? That of forgiver?

Not usually.

If you're like most people, the last thing you're thinking in these situations is how to forgive your offenders. Our initial response is anger. *How dare they!* We're usually thinking about the rotten thing they just did and how they should be punished. How we'd like them to feel the same way they just made us feel. How *we* can make them suffer. Eventually we calm down, but forgiveness isn't even the *second* thing on our minds. We want validation for our feelings, and we try to get that. We stew around, trying to make ourselves heard. We grumble until the next offense occurs, when the whole cycle starts over again.

But if we've made a decision to be a forgiver, we can no longer let the daily offenses pile up like we once did. We need to position our hearts to forgive. To position our hearts is to take a stance on forgiveness, to say to the world and everyone in it, "I choose to forgive rather than punish. I choose to forgive rather than become your victim. I choose to forgive rather than be a martyr. I choose to forgive and let go of the pain rather than internalize it and let it eat me up from the inside out."

When we position our hearts to forgive, we wake up each morning with the awareness that we may get our feelings hurt. We also know that when we do, we have a choice: We can internalize the pain and whine and complain, or we can forgive and let it go. The choice to forgive sometimes *involves* some whining and complaining, but if we have positioned our hearts to forgive, we will whine and complain less because we know that griping just prolongs the process.

The blame game doesn't stop just because we've positioned our heart to forgive. In fact, blaming is often part of the process of surrendering the pain. Hearing ourselves verbalize over and over again how awful so-and-so was to us can remind us of our need to let go of the offense. Then when others are hurting, we can let them go through the blaming stage as well.

Unfortunately, some people get stuck in the blame game. That's what you don't want to do—get stuck.

If our hearts are positioned to forgive, we are less likely to get stuck because we know that forgiveness is our goal each day. So when the airline loses our luggage, we may gripe and complain, but we know we need to let go of our anger and forgive the airline. When our hearts are positioned to forgive, we may write a very honest letter to our son's coach, but ultimately we know what we have to do—forgive him for not putting our son in the game as much as we think he should. The neighbor's dog does his thing in the yard one more time. Guess what's on our to-do list?

But if the offense is significant and the hurt deep, we may not know how we'll ever find it in ourselves to forgive. That's okay. Once we make an overall decision to be a forgiving person, God in his faithfulness orchestrates opportunities that will enable us to work through the pain and eventually find that place of compassion and mercy and forgiveness for the one who offended us.

Does positioning your heart to forgive mean you'll always love and forgive perfectly? Absolutely not. But you will see a definite difference in the way you process offenses done to you. You will begin to recognize the opportunities you have to forgive people, each and every day. On especially good days, you may not wait for obvious opportunities to come to you. Instead, you'll take advantage of the offenses committed by others who aren't even aware they've done anything at all.

"I forgive that guy for taking my parking place. I'll just go find another one."

"I forgive my son for playing his music so loud. I'll just wear my earplugs today and let him listen to it."

"I forgive my roommate for having his goofy friends over—again. I guess I'll just join the party."

Then a big opportunity to forgive comes along. I remember watching the news recently during a week of local protests in my city that resulted in a number of physical clashes between protesters and police. I found myself furious at the way the police were treating the protesters. Suddenly I heard myself telling a friend, "I hate the police." As I said those words, I remembered when the hatred had started—during the sixties and the Vietnam War protests, when I agonized as police beat protesters with batons, kicked them repeatedly when they were already on the ground, and killed the four students at Kent State. I hadn't realized I needed to forgive the police until I watched that news program that unleashed my anger. The police continued to confront protesters in my city while I confronted the unforgiveness within my heart.

When we are able to position our heart, to make the overall decision to be a forgiving person, with God's help we can start acting like forgivers.

*Ask Yourself*
Have I positioned my heart to forgive my world? How does that show itself in daily life?

Have I made the overall decision to relate to my world from a stance of mercy and compassion rather than bitterness and rancor? What does that look like in my current relationships?

Can I make a daily decision to let go of each and every offense that comes my way and see these as opportunities to once more extend God's forgiveness? What would help me do this on a more conscious level?

*To Do*
Make a list of all the pros and cons for and against a forgiving lifestyle. If we're holding on to pain and unforgiveness, it's because we're getting something out of it. Be as honest as you can. If punishing someone by not speaking to that person feels good to you, for instance, write it down on the "con" side of your list: "Sometimes it feels good to hold on to a grudge." Awareness is the first step toward making a change, and this list will make you aware of your reasons for either forgiveness or unforgiveness. When you've completed your list, take a hard look at who you are. Is this who you want to be?

# no longer stuck
# in revenge

When I returned to my car and found that someone had parked too close in front of me, boxing me in at both ends, I had the urge to bang their car about five times—hard. My car wasn't new; it could sustain some damage. But the one in front of me was a beaut—a cherry red sports car without any scratches. It hadn't been there when I'd parked a few hours earlier. Those little sports cars think they can squeeze in anywhere.

I didn't give in to my impulse that day (do you think I'd tell this story if I had?), but I can remember another time…

In his letter to the Romans, Paul wrote: "Do not take revenge, my friends, but leave room for God's wrath, for it is written: 'It is mine to avenge; I will repay,' says the Lord" (12:19). You know, if we saw any evidence of justice it would be one thing, but many times it appears as if God isn't doing anything to avenge us—at least not to the degree that we think he should—and so we're tempted to take matters into our own hands. We want revenge.

Most Christians I know feel guilty for desiring revenge on their enemies. Or on anyone else, for that matter. I know I've always felt guilty that I can't immediately pray for those who hurt me. Wish them good, not evil. Have compassion for whatever it was in them that caused them to attack me.

You'd think I'd eventually grow up in this area—you know, mature. I can understand wanting revenge when one is a child. Or a teenager. Or maybe even when one is in one's twenties and still not taking life all that seriously. But in one's thirties? Or forties? Give me a break. I'll be fifty pretty soon. Shouldn't I have learned to live with life's injustices by now? To move toward forgiveness rather than seek revenge when I'm wronged?

A few years ago my feelings of guilt were alleviated by something Dan Allender wrote in his book *Bold Love:* "Revenge involves a desire for justice. It is the intense wish to see ugliness destroyed, wrongs righted, and beauty restored. It is as inherent to the human soul as a desire for loveliness."[1] Allender goes on to say that the *desire for* revenge and the *action of inflicting* revenge on others are two different things. In other words, it's not wrong to desire revenge. In fact, it's part of being human; we all want justice. What's wrong—destructive—is taking justice into our own hands.

We get stuck in revenge when we become obsessed with demanding justice to the exclusion of everything else. "I didn't even recognize myself," one young man told me once. "I acted like a psycho, a crazy person. I wanted her to hurt as much as she'd hurt me." When his girlfriend had broken up with him to be in a relationship with someone who better met her needs, this normally shy and withdrawn young man turned into a crazed and jealous stalker. He wasn't able to share his deep hurt with his former girl-friend, so he internalized it and let it drive him to revenge. He not only stalked her, he took swings at her new boyfriend whenever he saw him.

There is only one answer to this man's deep hurt—forgiveness. He must forgive his girlfriend for dumping him, for not loving him anymore. It's that simple. He must acknowledge the hurt, grieve the loss of his girlfriend, and forgive her for not being what he needs. It's his only hope for experiencing the satisfying freedom of no longer being eaten up by the thirst for revenge.

For any of us, the only antidote for revenge is forgiveness.

When we agree to follow Jesus, we are agreeing to love and for-give one another. Both are part of the package of being a follower of Christ, yet sometimes we act as if we are ignorant of this. I can understand why. Forgiving others is hard, sometimes as hard as lov-ing them. That's because forgiving them *is* loving them.

When it comes to offering forgiveness rather than exacting revenge for wrongs done to us, Jesus is the ultimate example. He was the Son of God, come down from heaven to redeem us from ourselves. He was betrayed by one of his closest friends, publicly mocked, beaten, and ultimately crucified, simply for telling the truth about who he was. He could have inflicted revenge in any number of creative ways. Instead he prayed, "Father, forgive them, for they do not know what they are doing" (Luke 23:34).

We may protest, saying it's unfair to expect us to do what Jesus did because he was, after all, the Son of God. But he was also a man with human passions. I believe Jesus won the battle of forgive-ness not on the cross, but in the Garden of Gethsemane. In the garden Jesus was "sorrowful and troubled...to the point of death" (Matthew 26:37-38). He knew all the sufferings that lay ahead, including Judas's betrayal and his own death, and he prayed that the Father would take the cup of his crucifixion from him.

When we are troubled and upset because someone has mistreated us (or worse), we, too, must spend some time in the garden. Often, the deeper the wound, the deeper the desire for revenge. We must wrestle with our human feelings, with our calling to love and forgive, with our purpose to always take the higher road. As loyal followers of Christ, we will in time come to a place of fresh resolve and be able to say, "not my will, but yours be done" (Luke 22:42). It is in the garden that we win the battle over bitterness and revenge.

Sometimes the garden experience lasts for a while, maybe even for years. We pray, cry, and feel our hurt until finally we can think of our accuser without wanting to scream at, spit on, or shoot at someone or something—until we want to forgive.

We cannot love our world and simultaneously seek ways to take revenge for the wrongs done us. We have to choose one or the other.

## Ask Yourself

Have I been betrayed, wronged, hurt, abused, victimized? By whom? How do I feel about those violations now as I remember them?

Would I like the perpetrator to pay for what he or she did? Do I want anyone to hurt in the way I was hurt? If I'm honest, what do I think God should do with this person/these people?

How can I move my heart from the desire for revenge to the desire for forgiveness?

## To Do

Just for today, ask God to help you forgive everyone who has ever hurt you. Clean out your closet, so to speak. Get rid of the old (wounds, scars, bruises, aches, deformities) and make room for the new (forgiveness, love, compassion, mercy, care). Give up the desire for revenge just for one day. If it feels right, you may decide to give it up tomorrow, as well.

1. Dan Allender, *Bold Love* (Colorado Springs: NavPress, 1992), 187.

*Chapter Seven*

# in the absence
# of repentance

A few years ago I learned that my mother, with whom I'd had a painful love/hate relationship, was dying of cancer. Up until this time I had internalized the disappointment and hurt of our relationship, not knowing I could do anything else with these feelings. My pain would surface as rage on occasion, usually at those I loved the most—never at my mother. (Have you ever noticed that when someone wounds you, you strike out later at those who remind you of the perpetrator in some way?)

I was at my weekly prayer group, and a woman who knew of the situation asked me, "How would you like us to pray for your mother?"

Without hesitation I said, "Pray that she feels my love before she dies." I knew my mother didn't know that I loved her. How could she know? We weren't even speaking to one another.

The prayer was thrown into the mix of everything else on

God's to-do list. I didn't have much hope, but I did know the first step would have to be mine. I showed up at the hospital where I knew she'd be, aware she might not acknowledge my presence. It had happened before. One day I'd gone to her place of employment, and she had pretended she didn't even know me.

I took a big breath and entered her hospital room.

"Well hello there," she said.

"You've got so many flowers," I said in awe as I looked around the room. "A lot of people love you—"

"Oh yes," she groaned. "They come and line up along the walls with long faces. I don't know how I'm going to get these flowers home…"

She hadn't changed, she was still negative, still… I gulped, suddenly overcome with emotion. She just didn't know how to be any different. This was who she was, who she always had been.

My mom had seldom been there for me emotionally. Hardened by life, she was locked up inside of herself, unable to connect with anyone, including her own kids. I remember many times wanting her to comfort and hold me, only to be disappointed. The time she told me about my dad's death when I was five, for instance, and then just stoically watched me cry, not even reaching out to hold me. I don't think it was because she was mean; I think it was because *she* didn't feel anything.

Broken, I watched the old, bald, frail woman in front of me struggle to get into a comfortable position on the hospital bed. My mother was dying. Death has a way of putting things into perspective.

"Mom, I love you," I blurted, sobbing now.

"You do?" she said, surprised. "Well, I love you too."

No, that was too easy. I'd never heard her say those words

before. Now, just like that… What about all the things she'd done, all the neglect, the abandonment, her uncaring attitude toward any of my needs growing up, the…?

Should I try to elicit an apology from her? Now that we were speaking again, did I make my list of grievances and present it to her with a bow on top, add it to the gifts in her room that she still had to figure out how to take home—so that *I* would feel better?

I ran out of time to answer these questions. Mom died three weeks later. She never knew how much she'd hurt me.

In the days after my mother's death, the words of Jesus' prayer for his murderers kept running through my mind: "Father, forgive them, for they do not know what they are doing" (Luke 23:34).

It's true that some folks—even those closest to us—just never get it. I left my thirteen-year marriage because of physical, emotional, verbal, and spiritual abuse. Recently my ex-husband said to me, "Well, I know I must have done *something* to make you leave me." His brow creased slightly as he momentarily pondered what that might have been. It's been fifteen years since our divorce. He still doesn't get it.

When there is no validation, how do we move through the pain? How do we heal when there's no acknowledgment of sorrow or injustice? How do we forgive when there's no repentance?

Would it have been easier for Jesus to forgive those who crucified him if one of the Roman soldiers had stopped by the foot of the cross on his way to water the horses to say, "Oh by the way, I'm sorry we put you up there"? Would it have been easier for me if my mother had said the words that I wanted to hear? Maybe. I'm not sure. Either way, Jesus had to do the work in his heart. I had to do the work in my heart. You have to do the work in your heart.

The decision to forgive can never hinge on another person's

acknowledgment of a wrong done. Forgiveness is a gift: It is a gift to others because it sets them free from our judgment, and it is a gift to ourselves because it sets us free from bitterness and anger.

Until we understand this, we won't be motivated to forgive those who don't care whether they've hurt us. We offer the gift of forgiveness not because someone is sorry and so deserves our forgiveness, but because of who we are becoming as a lover and a forgiver in our world. Ultimately we have to see our offender through the eyes of compassion. This is what suddenly happened to me when I walked into my mother's hospital room. She was dying. How could I withhold love and forgiveness from her one minute longer?

But what if someone isn't dying? They're alive and well and harassing you continually. For the most part, I don't think people are aware of how they harass others—enough reason for compassion right there. If they *are* aware and still do it, I would say they deserve our compassion more than anyone else. Do they ever need some help!

How do we cultivate a heart of compassion? Simple. By choosing to be a forgiver. If we truly want to follow Jesus' example and forgive rather than demand vengeance, we must take all the injustices done to us and choose to forgive—not simply for the sake of the relationship, but for the larger purpose of loving our world.

*Ask Yourself*

Who has hurt me yet never acknowledged it? Whom have I not forgiven because of this?

Can I exercise the courage and do the internal work necessary to begin the forgiveness process without any sign of remorse from that person? Where do I have to start inside of myself, what do I have to remember, how can I perceive the situation and this person in a different light in order to have compassion?

Can I offer the gift of forgiveness, in a much larger sense, not to a person but for the purpose of following Christ and loving my world?

*To Do*

Think about who has wronged you and never taken any kind of responsibility for it. Write this person a letter that you may or may not send. Downplay the wrongs done to you, and emphasize your part in working through the forgiveness process so that you can still be available to God as a lover of your world.

# do it for yourself

"What do you want to do?" I asked my friend as she vacillated between two seemingly right decisions.

"What do *I* want to do?" She looked at me, obviously puzzled. "What do you mean?"

I looked back at her, just as puzzled. Couldn't she answer this simple question? "Just what I said. What do *you* want to do?"

She shrugged. "Well, I don't know. I've…no one has ever asked me that before." Then she told me that her entire Christian life was focused on what others wanted; she'd never before considered what she wanted. This was a new concept for her.

This woman isn't unusual. As females and as Christians, many of us have spent our lives doing what those around us want—spouses, friends, parents, kids, or bosses/coworkers. We are so focused on what others want that we don't know what *we* want.

Perhaps no one has ever asked us—and it never occurred to us to ask ourselves.

What does knowing what you want have to do with choosing a lifestyle of forgiveness? Everything! I've learned that it's not worthwhile to do something just because it's the right thing to do. Unless I am choosing to forgive because I want to forgive, I become resentful; I feel like I'm not being true to myself or that I'm being taken advantage of. But when I forgive from my heart, I act out of a place of integrity. You and I must cultivate a habit of forgiveness not because God requires it or because that is what good Christians do, but because we want to...because deep in our hearts we know that God only asks of us things that are ultimately for our good.

When we offer forgiveness to another person, we reap the greater benefit. Living a lifestyle of forgiveness means that no matter what the offense, we will take the time and energy we need in order to forgive the one who hurt us. No matter whether there's sorrow or repentance on the part of the offender. No matter if the relationship has to change or end because the offender is unable or unwilling to stop wounding us. We forgive because this is the way we've chosen to live our lives.

Are you reading this book because forgiveness is something you think you should do—or because you want to be a forgiving person?

Becoming that kind of person isn't easy. What if you think a lifestyle of forgiveness means getting walked on? What if you've forgiven in the past and feel like it's gotten you nowhere? What if you believe in forgiveness but never consciously practice it? How can you get to the place where you *want* to live a forgiving lifestyle?

I've heard life manager Phil McGraw say that we often behave in negative ways because we get something out of that behavior.

We get some kind of payback. Otherwise, we could easily change our behavior. We need to identify what it is that keeps us from forgiving, what we're getting out of holding on to unforgiveness. Could it be that an unforgiving heart feeds that dark place in us that cries out for revenge? Could it be that staying mad is less painful than feeling the sadness over the offense done to us? Could it be that we're just much too busy and/or lazy to do the hard work forgiveness requires in our hearts?

I've been at this forgiveness thing for a few years now, and it's some of the hardest internal work I've ever done. Sometimes it's a matter of gritting my teeth and forgiving in spite of my mean and spiteful self. But when I make the decision to forgive even when I don't feel like it, I'm reminded once again of the transforming power of God that lies within me, his child. Convinced that God calls me to forgive, and because it benefits me in ways that hanging on to the pain never does, I go to him for help.

As I write these words, I'm thinking of a woman I'm in the process of forgiving. Every so often I try out scenarios in my imagination to see if I've completed the forgiveness process. I imagine hugging her and saying, "I forgive you," even though I can see her scoffing at me. I know she doesn't think she did anything she needs forgiveness for. That's okay. We don't offer forgiveness to others because they think they need it. That's not the point. We offer forgiveness because we know we need to. In order to go on. In order to grow. In order not to let bitterness take root in our hearts. In order to be the kind of loving, caring people of God who can change the world, one forgiving person at a time.

I believe that God presents us with opportunities to forgive someone every single day. Most of us think about forgiveness only in terms of those with whom we are in relationship, but I believe that when God calls us to forgive others, he's calling us to something beyond our front door—literally.

One recent evening I came home to find a strange car parked in my parking spot. *My* parking spot. Grrrrr. I had to park two spaces farther away from my front door. Even more aggravating, I could see by looking at the number of cars parked in front of the house next door that the car belonged to someone there, not to someone in my apartment complex. How dare they! I marched into my apartment and groused for a while.

In time I recognized I had two options: I could search out the culprit and demand that he move his car, or I could forgive him for being inconsiderate of me. Mine was such a simple problem, really, especially when I consider the homeless sleeping under bridges a few short miles from my home in Seattle. Not only do they not have cars to park, they have no food or shelter.

I forgave the driver of the car and wished him well as he partied next door.

And you know what? I was much happier for it.

Yes, I know forgiveness is not always that simple. But thank God, sometimes it is. These smaller, often daily, opportunities to forgive prepare us for the bigger times when it's more than someone stepping on our toes.

God is standing by, working with you and for you as you seek his help in becoming a person of forgiveness. Forgiveness is for *you* more than it is for the person you forgive. And you're worth the trouble, don't you think?

## Ask Yourself

In all honesty, do I see how forgiveness benefits me, even if I can't see any visible results in anyone else's life? Can I forgive others because of the benefits I might receive? Is that enough, or do I need a higher purpose?

How can I get to the place where I recognize that a lifestyle of forgiveness is something I need to do because ultimately it is good for me?

## To Do

The next time someone offends you in any way, bypass the "Oh, I shouldn't be hurt, that's silly, I'm too sensitive" stage and go directly to forgiveness. Offer forgiveness because you know it will bring the healing that God desires for you. You're worth it. Watch for that opportunity today.

*Chapter Nine*

# forgiving
# yourself

An inability to forgive others often stems from an inability to forgive ourselves. When we withhold forgiveness from others, it's usually because we can't face the fact that we, too, need forgiveness. We don't want to see the truth about how "bad" we are, so we deny our "badness," thereby erasing our need for forgiveness.

What do we need to forgive ourselves for?

- "stupid" mistakes
- hurting others
- poor decisions
- human weaknesses
- succumbing to temptation
- self-absorption

And that's just for starters!

This week a Seattle newspaper reported two separate tragedies of fathers who had never forgiven themselves. Both dads took their own lives after killing their children because they feared their sons carried the same flawed genes as were in themselves. One lived in Washington and the other in Georgia. In their suicide notes both fathers confessed that they wouldn't allow their sons to grow up to become losers, as they had been. They wanted to save them from that future. Obviously, these men made some terrible mistakes in their lives to have come to such a conclusion. If they could have taken responsibility for the behavior that caused them to feel like losers, if they had understood even a bit about God's mercy, they might have received his forgiveness and then entered into the process of forgiving themselves.

Granted, these examples are extreme. But all of us lash out at others when we don't forgive ourselves. For example, if we were sexually involved as teenagers, we may become hyper-vigilant with our children because we fear they will do what we did—or worse. At the first sign that our fears might be coming true, we react with judgment and condemnation, thereby preventing honest and much-needed dialogue. Our inability or refusal to forgive ourselves eventually affects our current relationships as well as our perception of anyone who comes across our path.

Part of the problem is that when we blame others for the messes we get in, we avoid seeing the need to forgive ourselves. After all, if we are not responsible for what happens to us, we never have anything to forgive ourselves for. (I used to pull out this excuse from my bag of tricks whenever anyone tried to hold me accountable for something I'd done, using it as a shield.) Another form of blaming occurs when we play the role of victim and/or martyr. Victims believe that someone really did hurt them, so they don't have to look at themselves. The problem lies with the other person, not them.

One indication that we might need to forgive ourselves is an inability to move beyond a particular incident as signaled by our constant conversation about it, especially about how bad we feel. When we haven't been able to get past something, it's often because we haven't forgiven ourselves. For example, I can become self-righteous and judgmental when it comes to self-righteous and judgmental people. When this happens, I know it's a sign that once again I need to forgive myself for the many years I approached life from a self-righteous and judgmental stance. I remember, for instance, telling my mother that she was "going to hell" if she didn't give up Catholicism and become a "Christian," as if a person couldn't be both. No wonder there was a bit of a breach in our relationship after that.

To forgive ourselves is to let ourselves off the hook, to quit punishing ourselves and wake up to the fact that we are human with human weaknesses and frailties. We do a terrible disservice to others when we elevate ourselves above them simply because we have chosen to follow Jesus Christ and they have not. If you're having a hard time finding anything to forgive yourself for, you might start by making a list of all of those times you have, because of your faith, thought of yourself as better than someone else.

We've all done it. Someone says or does something and we think, *I would never have said such a thing* or *I would never have done it that way.* "Do not think of yourself more highly than you ought, but rather think of yourself with sober judgment, in accordance with the measure of faith God has given you" (Romans 12:3). I take this to mean we are supposed to view or evaluate ourselves only according to how we're applying our faith in everyday life.

Do we think we know something? "Knowledge puffs up, but

love builds up. The man who thinks he knows something does not yet know as he ought to know. But the man who loves God is known by God" (1 Corinthians 8:1-3). In other words, what we know is not what is important. What's important to God is how we love.

Do we think we're something special compared to everyone else? "If anyone thinks he is something when he is nothing, he deceives himself. Each one should test his own actions. Then he can take pride in himself, without comparing himself to somebody else, for each one should carry his own load" (Galatians 6:3-5).

Jesus had a lot of harsh things to say about the self-righteousness of the Pharisees. I believe many Christians today (me included) have been guilty of the same spiritual pride. We have placed ourselves above those who don't follow Christ instead of coming alongside people as fellow seekers and sojourners. In doing so, we have alienated the very ones we had hoped to reach.

When we neglect to forgive ourselves, we are saying no to God's gift, the gift that he extends to us freely and mercifully, no matter what we've done. Yes, he forgives us unconditionally. But the process is complete only when we take his forgiveness and apply it to ourselves.

Now you know more than you ever wanted to know about how we avoid the hard work of forgiving ourselves in order to ultimately receive God's forgiveness so we can forgive others. I hope you've gotten the message that learning to forgive yourself is an important step in cultivating a daily habit of forgiveness. Go easy on yourself. Learn to deal with yourself with the kind of compassion with which God deals with you.

*Ask Yourself*

How have I elevated myself above others in any way at all—spiritually, emotionally, intellectually?

Do I ever think I'm at a higher level than other people, know more than other people, am more than other people? How does this affect my daily relationships?

Can I call this what it is—self-righteousness? What do I need to forgive myself for when it comes to self-righteousness?

*To Do*

Whether you think of yourself as better than others or less than others, the emphasis is still on you. Whether you think of yourself as victim or martyr, it's all about the heavy cross you are bearing. Today, know that you are a part of God's bigger picture, and that in order to truly carry your cross (which by the way, is not a heavy one—Matthew 11:30), you must join the team. What specific step can you take to bring yourself down a notch before someone else does?

*Chapter Ten*

# forgiving God

God never sins. He never makes mistakes. Everything he does is perfect. Why would he need our forgiveness?

He doesn't. The need is ours. We need to forgive him—for failing to come through for us in the way we thought he would, for not giving us what we asked for, for allowing those we love to suffer and die in spite of our prayers for healing—because when these "offenses" begin to pile up, our love relationship with God grows distant. We back away, hurt and angry that God "didn't come through for us." At least, that's how it seems.

It was a startling reality to me to discover I was mad at God. Ticked off is putting it way too mildly. Furious would be more like it. I was enraged. Even though I hadn't had any direct communication with God for a while (a sure sign that something had gone awry), I wasn't even aware of my anger until my friend Katie's wedding.

I knew when I first received the wedding invitation that I didn't want to go. I didn't want to be anywhere near that church on my friend's wedding day. Not only that, but when I found out she was getting married, I didn't want to be anywhere near my friend, either. I'd do anything to avoid her in the halls at work. What was wrong with me?

"C-c-congratulations," I managed to squeak out one day right after she told me her news.

"Thanks," she said, but she was looking at me with an odd expression. Katie is one of my more perceptive friends.

I ducked into my office and avoided her after that.

I didn't think about it much until the day of the wedding; I couldn't think of an excuse not to go. She'd baby-sat my kids many times, and of course they wanted to see their big sister–friend get married. So, we got all dressed up and went to the wedding, where I proceeded to gag all the way through the beautiful ceremony.

The guilt was really strong now. I was choking on it. Or was there something else that had a stranglehold on me? Suddenly I knew what it was: grief over my own failed marriage. I'd been only nineteen years old when I married my ex-husband, and I had been a Christian for only a month. I believe now that I was actually looking for a father figure. I married a man who was fifteen years older than I was and who loved the role of authority figure that I'd quite easily handed over to him. I'd never prayed about getting married, about whom I should marry, about anything. I'd just impulsively decided one day to do it.

I somehow made it through my friend's wedding ceremony and then back home, where I literally ran for the bathroom off my bedroom away from the rest of the house and screamed out the pain I had repressed for years. "God, how could you have let me marry someone who would hit me?" I was sobbing now. "What were you thinking, knowing what he would do and how it would affect me and the kids? And they say you're a loving God? All those years of my life—just wasted."

I was angry, really angry—for what I perceived as God's neglect, his turning his head while the abuse took place, his being preoccupied somewhere else. Worst of all, for his watching while it happened.

But in the next moment I felt God's presence with me in the bathroom. "I never intended for you or your children to get beat up," he seemed to say. "I didn't create men with strength so they could beat up on women. I gave them strength so they could protect their wives and their children from predators—humans and animals—and so they could go to battle and win in the war over evil."

Was I making this up? The words made so much sense.

My anger began to subside over the next several weeks, and I realized how much I'd missed God, hearing his tender voice in my heart, feeling his nudges to move in a certain direction and his concern for every aspect of my life. This breakthrough eventually caused me to see, of course, that my heavenly Father had been there all along—I just needed to recognize him as such.

It seems presumptuous to say we need to forgive the Creator for anything—anything at all. But sometimes we build up a view of God that is so faulty and full of holes that when he acts outside the parameters of our perception, we become confused and sometimes, as in my case, enraged. We all have very personal and sometimes desperate needs. In our immaturity we place expectations on God to meet those needs in a way that we have specifically mapped out, whether consciously or unconsciously. These expectations often turn into demands, and when he doesn't come through for us in the way we want him to, we can become depressed and enraged.

In my case, I thought God should have prevented me from getting married. And he certainly should not have let my husband abuse me.

When we're angry at God, we usually can't acknowledge our anger at first. It's terrifying to think that we may have a problem with the way God's running the universe—and our lives in particular. So we pretend. On the outside our relationship with God looks good—we pray, attend church, read the Bible, mouth all the right spiritual clichés around our Christian friends. But inside a slow burn is starting. This slow burn eventually grows into a raging fire, like mine did the day of the wedding.

Unfortunately, most of us feel so guilty for our anger toward God that we seldom admit it, and so we never make it to forgiveness. Our spiritual life becomes a fantasy, built on sandcastles of hopes, dreams, and longings that we believe God will someday fulfill. We cling to this fantasy tenaciously, becoming enraged at anyone who dares to challenge it. We direct our rage at any scapegoat we can find, venting our fury.

What we really need to do is slump down against a wall and cry our guts out, forgiving God for the unfulfilled hopes, dreams, and longings. We need to let go of our demands for all that we once deemed so possible and so imminent, but now know will never be achieved. Unless we grieve their passing and forgive God for what we see as a terrible injustice, we can't build new hopes, create new dreams, and hold new longings. We will be forever stuck in a clogged channel of unforgiveness, us on one side, God on the other, both of us unable to reach the other.

Forgiving God means getting honest with ourselves in order to see that the expectations we have placed on him are just that—our expectations. It means letting God be God—accepting that he has his own way of doing things and trusting whatever that ends up looking like in our lives. It means that much of what we see as *God* doing something is really *us* doing something—and getting ourselves in a terrible jam. It means taking responsibility for our own lives. It means narrowing our expectations down to one and only one thing—God loves us.

God is always there to love, redeem, and heal.

## Ask Yourself

What might I be holding against God? What in my life do I think
is terribly unfair?

How do I believe God could have fixed it? Made my life better?
Where do I see that God let me down?

Can I find it in my heart to forgive God for the perceived disappointments and injustices in my life?

## To Do

Forgiving God means having a heart-to-heart talk. He knows
what's in your heart, but he won't force you to share it. Choose
today to unclog the channels, to clear the sludge, to forgive a God
who never meant for you to be hurt, who grieves even more than
you do at the injustices and disappointments you've suffered, who
longs to give you new hopes, dreams, and longings. Write him a
letter, listing all the times you wanted him to be there and wondered where he was, all the times you felt alone, feeling like he had
bigger and better things to do than watch over you. When you fin-
ish your list, cry, scream, do whatever it takes for you to access the
forgiveness you have in your heart.

*Chapter Eleven*

# no condemnation

I remember a certain celebrity whose son died from a drug overdose. He went on every talk show and made a ton of TV commercials. His face kept appearing on magazine covers. His message was always the same: "We have to get drug dealers off the streets; they're killing our kids."

Now in theory, he may have a point. But the fact is, his son had a free will; he purchased and took the drugs all by himself. Yet every time I heard this father talk, he went on and on about how awful the guy was who gave his son the drugs. This went on for years. Annoyed with his bitter tone and his angry expressions, I remember thinking, *Get over it already. You think your kid wasn't in any way responsible—or that he's the only one who's ever died from a drug overdose? Exercise some forgiveness and get on with your life!*

All of us fall into the trap of condemning others. Sometimes our condemnation is communicated when we bluntly state our opinion to another person: "Don't you think it's about time you and so-and-so got your issues resolved? You've been sitting on opposite sides of the church now for over two months." At other times it takes a more subtle tone: "I saw your sister the other day; she sure feels bad about the breach between the two of you. I'm so glad I worked things out with my brother before he died last year."

We might genuinely care about how another person is working through the forgiveness process. Nothing wrong with that. We may even have definite opinions about what that person should be doing to move the process along and heal the relationship. Nothing wrong with that, either. But what is wrong is criticizing that person for not being where we think he or she should be. That's where I stepped over the line with the celebrity whose son died of a drug overdose. My patience with him ran out. I decided he had grieved long enough and now he needed to forgive and get on with things—basically so I didn't have to listen to his pain anymore.

But maybe this father *was* getting on with his life. Maybe he was doing the best he could. Who am I to decide how much time another person needs to forgive? We're all doing the best we can, aren't we?

Can we believe that about the people who hurt us and then leave the rest to God? He's the one who works in people's hearts. We can remind him that things could be done in a more timely manner, but we really have no control in this arena. We might as well accept that. If someone's process of forgiveness takes months or years, it's between that person and God.

Forgiveness is a delicate and fragile process, and God is the one who orchestrates it—in his time. He's the one who knows when another person is ready. Not me. Not you. God. He created each of us. Whenever we become irritated and condemning because we think a person is too slow to forgive, we need to realize that we're really criticizing God for the way he made that person.

Condemnation from others is incredibly painful. I've watched more than one of our brothers and sisters back away, avoid, and finally drop out of church and Bible studies because of Christians there who kept telling them where they should be in their forgiveness process. When a person is already in pain because of a broken relationship and then is judged for not being further along in the process by those who claim to love him or her—well, it's just more than some people can bear.

I'm not saying I've never condemned anyone. I have. But I've told God that I don't want to, and I've asked him to change my attitudes. If we really believe that God is sovereign and works in people's hearts, then maybe we need to shut our mouths and pray that God will help them find their way. Difficult to do when we think we know the best way, of course...

I've certainly had times when I moved slowly through the forgiveness process, and even though others questioned whether I genuinely wanted to be forgiving, I felt God's presence and assurance that my timing was perfect. God alone knows our hearts. When we are in the forgiveness process, he is with us, watching over the process. He is always moving and creating and growing us up. It's not in his nature to sit still. While he may not be condemning us for taking our time, we can trust that he is always nudging us through the process. I'm forever feeling his gentle push from behind: "What about Kelly? Don't you have some unfinished business? Or Jason? Remember what he said to you last week and how you felt? How do you feel about him today?"

These are questions I'm not always eager to answer or even think about. But I know that if I said, "Later, God," he would leave me alone—but he'd be back. So I usually deal with his nudges the first time. It's easier.

We're the ones who make it so hard on ourselves. We think we have to do it perfectly—and do it now. Keep this in mind: When we condemn ourselves, we are using up the energy that we could be putting into moving the forgiveness process forward. The end result is that it takes even longer to forgive.

It boils down to trust. When we condemn ourselves or another person for not moving forward in forgiveness, we are not trusting that God is at work in that person's life. Just because we can't always see any visible movement doesn't mean it's not happening. If we can remind ourselves that God is the one in charge, we can relax, continue to pray for ourselves and others who are in the forgiveness process, and trust that God will bring about the healing in his time.

Condemnation—whether from ourselves or others—is simply a big, fat distraction. Nothing productive ever comes out of it. Learn to look for it so you can put your energy into what really matters: reaching out in love and compassion to offer one of God's greatest gifts to another person—the gift of forgiveness.

## Ask Yourself

Am I condemning anyone for how he or she is managing or even avoiding the process of forgiveness? Who? Can I dig a little deeper inside myself for the compassion that I know is there and let go of my feelings of condemnation?

Am I feeling condemned for my inability to forgive someone? How does that feeling block the process of forgiveness in my life and relationships?

Can I let go of what others think about how I'm managing my forgiveness process? Can I let go of my condemning perception of how others manage theirs?

Where am I when it comes to trust? Can I trust that God is moving even when I can't see any visible signs?

## To Do

Write a note or e-mail someone today and tell him or her you're proud of the way he or she is handling a difficult relationship, that you know forgiveness is a process and takes courage. Commit to do your best to stop condemning others for their way of moving through their pain, no matter how long it takes.

*Chapter Twelve*

# measuring
# your steps

A particular photo has become uncomfortably familiar to many Americans, even though it pictures an event that occurred over thirty years ago. It shows a young, naked Vietnamese girl running for her life after her village was bombed. She had just ripped off her burning clothes, and the photographer was able to shoot her straight on as she screamed in anguish and terror.

Now a grown woman, she was interviewed recently. When asked if she had the photo hanging in her house anywhere, she said no, that it was still hard to see and think about that day. But she was able to talk about it now, to answer questions.

"I am learning how to forgive the people who caused my suffering," she said.

"Really?!" the interviewer exclaimed, obviously surprised.

"Yes. I tell you that it was the fire of bomb that burned my body," she went on in her broken English. "It was skill of doctors

73

that mended my skin. But it took power of God's love to heal my heart."

Even though the event still brings up pain, the fact that this woman could talk about it indicates that she has moved forward in the forgiveness process. Just because we haven't completely forgiven those who hurt us doesn't mean we aren't growing in forgiveness. The process is sometimes one agonizing step after another. Forgiveness rarely occurs as a one-time event; it often takes place in stages.

Our reactions and feelings usually indicate where we are in the forgiveness process. In the early years of my Christian growth, I used to condemn and berate myself when my reactions to those who had hurt me revealed that I hadn't yet completed the forgiveness process, even when I thought I had. I didn't know then that forgiveness takes time and that these "negative" reactions can be good things if we pay attention to them. They can point out that we still have work to do.

Here are some reactions that may be signals that you have more work to do:

- the offense still troubles you, often and regularly
- the memory of the offense evokes pain
- thoughts of the person who caused the offense provoke anger
- you avoid a person or situation because of uncomfortable or hostile feelings

I remember being deeply hurt by a couple of friends, telling them I forgave them, and then for months afterward feeling the pain every time I saw a car that looked like one of theirs. Unfortunately, they owned Volkswagens, popular cars, and so I was encountering this pain way too often for my comfort. It finally occurred to me that I was still in the middle of the process; I hadn't completely forgiven my friends. The day finally came when I could see a yellow or red Volkswagen and not feel pain—nor did I even remember that my friends owned similar cars. My forgiveness process was complete.

If our goal is to develop a daily lifestyle of forgiveness, we need to monitor our feelings—every day. Even though forgiveness, like love, is a choice, it has many feelings connected to it. And these feelings, like good friends, can remind us of our commitment to be forgiving, to relate to our world in forgiving ways.

Most of us are confronted every day—at work, at home, around those we love the most—with opportunities to monitor where we are in the forgiveness process. You may think you've forgiven that coworker who took credit for your idea last week, but now you find yourself undermining him to both your boss and other coworkers in little ways. Are you still angry at him? Have you *really* forgiven him?

Or maybe you're late for a meeting and you run out to the car only to find the gas gauge on empty—again. Remembering all the other times he's done this, you feel a rush of anger toward your son. Your anger is understandable, but you still need to forgive your son. Your response can tell you if you have.

You won't always feel like forgiving immediately, even when you see the need to do so. You may need to have a talk with someone or get alone with God to express some feelings. That's okay. What's important is that you begin to recognize that you need to forgive someone—and that you make the choice to forgive as soon as your heart is ready. Offering forgiveness should be an item not on our annual planner, but on our daily to-do list.

Sometimes we ignore our hurt feelings, thinking we're doing ourselves and those with whom we live a favor. After all, we should be beyond getting hurt over every little thing. But many times those we think of as "supersensitive" are people who have stashed their hurt feelings over the years, building them up until there is such a huge pile the feelings are coming out everywhere—usually in snappy and irritated tones and occasional rages. These are not bitter, unforgiving souls as much as they are hurting, suffering souls who need to acknowledge and experience God's healing grace.

What I'm about to suggest may seem a little crazy, since it means signing up for pain, but we can ask God for more opportunities to keep moving and growing in forgiveness. Like the Vietnamese woman, we can say yes to remembering. This woman didn't have to give that interview. Now that she lives in a different country, she could closet away the memories and everything associated with that trauma in her past and never deal with them again. But her demeanor and attitude proved to me that she is more committed to growth than she is to comfort. I believe she agreed to the interview, knowing it would bring up painful memories for her, because she knew her journey through forgiveness might inspire others watching to embark on a journey of their own.

Forgiveness is a complex process. We alone know where we've been, the injustices we've suffered. We alone know whom we need to forgive and for what. The most precious gift we can give ourselves and those we care about is to stay in touch with our deepest feelings so that we can keep growing and forgiving. God is always waiting, available to help us make it to yet the next step in the process.

## Ask Yourself

Is there any person the mention of whose name brings up hurt for me? Is there anyone I avoid because of the hurt and/or angry feelings I experience around him or her? Any situation I purposely avoid?

Do I need to talk to anyone to see if I can get validation, to see if I can move any closer to forgiving that person or group of people?

What or whom do I still need to grieve in order to keep moving through the forgiveness process?

## To Do

Practice forgiveness today. If you're alive, you get hurt. We all do. Let yourself feel the feelings of a recent hurt. Is it connected to anything in the past, an offense committed by either that same person or someone else? As you grieve the pain, let yourself feel compassion for the suffering of the offender. Now forgive that person or group of people, assuring yourself that they "don't know what they're doing." Remember Jesus' words: "You will grieve, but your grief will turn to joy" (John 16:20). The act of forgiving is a transforming one; it changes you.

*Chapter Thirteen*

# embracing
# the fear

One reason we resist or avoid forgiving others, even though we
know it's the right thing to do, is the unconscious fear that rises up
when we try to move forward. We're afraid of:

- putting ourselves in a position where the one who hurt us
  might do so again
- reexperiencing the original pain
- diminishing the awfulness of the offense by forgiving
- giving up the role of victim and the attention accompany-
  ing that role

There may be more, but these are the biggies. The more we
dwell on the fear, the bigger it gets until it paralyzes us. If it's true
that forgiveness is a gift, we simply have to open up our hearts and
receive it. This can't happen when we're paralyzed, tightly holding
on to our fear.

As a new Christian, I believed that if I felt afraid, I couldn't be walking in God's love. I thought that if I was afraid, I was out of God's will and God was displeased with me. I know better now. Being afraid isn't a sin, nor is God unhappy with us when we're afraid. Our fear is simply a state of being that reveals that our love is not yet perfected. "There is no fear in love. But perfect love drives out fear" (1 John 4:18). If we can acknowledge our fear, God's power in us to love can be released.

In other words, fear can be our teacher, guiding us in our personal growth and showing us what we need to pay attention to. If we're afraid, we can start asking questions that will eventually lead us to answers that will help us grow in our relationships with others.

This was true for a young woman I once knew who couldn't forgive her stepbrother for the years of ridicule and teasing he had heaped on her as they were growing up. She would recount over and over to anyone who would listen how awful her life had been, how she had low self-esteem because of her stepbrother's treatment, how she couldn't relate to men because of him—in fact, she blamed him for every dysfunction in her life.

What he had done was wrong, it's true, and her friends and other family members sympathized with her until a particularly perceptive friend confronted her one day. "You like playing the role of victim. You're *afraid* to forgive your stepbrother because you'll have to give up that role. It gets you the attention you're craving." This conversation caused her to ask some hard questions. Was she using the situation as an excuse to keep from growing? If she forgave her stepbrother, how would her life change? What reason would she have then for her low self-esteem and her unhealthy relationships with men? The answers to these questions revealed to her what she needed to do to move past those problems.

How do you recognize fear? What does it look like? It often creeps in when you're in the process of grieving the pain connected to the offense, so you don't notice it. If you're having a problem for-giving someone, simply ask yourself what you're afraid of. I may be stepping out on a limb here, but I would say that fear may be 100 percent underneath your inability to forgive.

Unfortunately, some of us don't face our fears precisely because we're afraid to! We fear (verb) fear (noun), if you know what I mean. For me, the very act of admitting my fear makes me incred-ibly anxious. The admission of fear says I'm a wuss, I can't handle whatever it is, I need help, blah, blah, blah…none of which I want anyone to know. I want others to think I'm strong, that I can handle anything. If I admit my fear, someone or something (who knows what or who—a monster?) will swoop down and say, "Ha, I knew it—you're afraid. Now I'll get you." Lately I've been better—when I'm afraid, I can at least say to God in a little tiny voice, "God, I'm kind of scared of this. If I forgive so-and-so, this or that might happen." I know now that the best way to deal with my fear is to not only admit it but embrace it. And how do you embrace fear? You welcome it into your life as a teacher. You don't condemn, berate, or scold yourself for what you see as fear. You understand that it is present to teach you something about wisdom, about yourself, about God and his compassion.

I'm not saying that embracing fear is easy. It's not. Fear doesn't just go away. It's like this iguana my daughter once had. I swear, every time I walked in and out of her bedroom—which I admit was less often once the iguana took up residence there—the thing had doubled in size. If we keep ignoring our fears, especially the ones connected to our inability to forgive, they get bigger. And we become bitter and hostile. Like the woman who couldn't forgive her stepbrother, we start making excuses for not forgiving and then start blaming others for our problems.

"I'm this way because so-and-so abused me when I was twelve."

"I act like that because I was fired from my job in 1976."

"I can't do that because someone took advantage of me the last time I did it."

How do you let go of fear? You replace it with compassion and mercy for your offender. You may have to do this many times over. Fear usually leaves in stages, and sometimes we're not even aware that it's gone until we once again experience the situation that so often caused us fear—and we realize it's no longer there.

Another thing: When we are able to embrace the fear connected to the process of forgiveness—whatever that fear might be—we are choosing to walk in compassion toward another person or other persons.

Forgiveness doesn't mean I have to hang around that person every day or even once a week. In fact, I may choose never to see that person again—ever. But when I think of him or her, I can do so without hostility or animosity. My thoughts are no longer emotionally charged with hurtful memories and offenses. I am able to go on and let the other person go on.

Living free from paralyzing fear is always the goal; the paradox is that we can only do that when we first embrace the fear and make it our teacher.

*Ask Yourself*
What are the fears I have connected to my avoidance of forgiveness? Do I know myself well enough to identify them?

Why do I think I might be letting my fear(s)—rather than the desire to forgive—control me?

Can I embrace my fears, let go of them, and begin to play a new role, a role other than victim?

*To Do*
Once you've identified your fears, create an approach to deal with them directly. It may mean humbling yourself in front of others, confronting someone, or taking seriously what others think is no big deal at all. Only you know what's going on inside you. Only you know whom you need to forgive.

*Chapter Fourteen*

# an act of
# courage

Forgiveness takes a great deal of courage. It's always easier to hang on to our pain and disappointment, withdraw our love, and try to make others suffer. Forgiveness requires us to confront the pain of the offense. This is true whether the offense is as "small" as giving up our right to a certain lane on the freeway or as "big" as listening to our offender's pain and offering compassion when we ourselves are full of unexpressed pain. The ability to forgive is always available to us, but we are the ones who decide whether we'll be courageous enough to receive the gift.

One reason forgiveness takes courage is that it requires vulnerability. Any time we are vulnerable, we open ourselves up to pain.

About a year ago, a friend of mine attended a fiftieth wedding anniversary celebration for her aunt and uncle. Relatives were there from both sides of the family—something especially meaningful to this couple and their children because the aunt's family had boycotted the wedding fifty years before. Her father was adamantly opposed to the marriage and had forbidden any of his children to attend the ceremony. Even though many of them were grown and had families of their own, they felt they needed to honor their father's wishes. No one from the aunt's side of the family had come to the wedding.

As part of the anniversary celebration, this woman retold the story of her wedding and the feelings of abandonment and rejection surrounding that day. With tears, she also spoke of the joy she felt at that moment because all had been forgiven, as evidenced by the presence of the woman's siblings at this fiftieth wedding anniversary. It was a day of celebration.

Or so the aunt thought. Even before the celebration ended, her brothers and sisters were talking among themselves about how inappropriate it was for her to talk about their father "that way." When their sister finally learned of their reaction, she was at first appalled and then deeply hurt. Tragically, instead of understanding her intent to celebrate and continue to forgive, her siblings judged her words as disrespectful, damaging, and unnecessary.

The forgiveness process requires courage. This woman's need to retell the story of her pain in order to continue to heal and move forward in forgiveness took tremendous courage on her part. But it was rejected and misunderstood by the very people who could have helped her the most. No, moving ahead in forgiveness is not always easy.

Look around you. Do you have an opportunity to exercise the courage to forgive? When those who have experienced sexual abuse, male or female, are getting in touch with issues surrounding the abuse, it takes courage to forgive their abusers. It can't be rushed or manipulated. They must exercise courage on their terms, in their own way, in their own time.

On a smaller scale, but no less scary, is confronting another person with an offense in order to protect the relationship. I'm trying to do this more, but it doesn't seem to get any easier. Every time, I have to take a deep breath and pray for courage. Why? Because when someone hurts me, deliberately or otherwise, I assume they don't care. If I say something, make an "issue" out of it, I know I will probably discover whether or not I'm right—and I'm not always sure I want to know.

If you're not used to exercising courage this way, here are some tips that may help:

- Look at your options. (1) You can hang on to the offense, big or little, and let it slowly eat away at you until you're a bitter and angry person. (2) You can confront your offender and hope for validation. (3) You can vent to a therapist and hope the therapist is good enough to guide you to a place of healing. (4) You can grow in courage so that forgiveness becomes not an option but a necessary step in your spiritual growth.

- Remember that fear always precedes courage. In order to exercise courage, you must first experience fear. This is one reason, as we discovered in the last chapter, that you can view fear as your teacher.

- Courage grows as we exercise it. But we have to start. "I choose to forgive rather than punish." We may not feel it the first time we say it. That's okay. We don't always have to feel our convictions in order to act on them. Do you believe in the power of forgiveness? Do you believe that it's what God wants for you in your relationships? Do you believe you'll be a better person for having learned how to forgive? This is all you need.

- We often have to take the first step before the courage comes. We may not feel courageous. We may feel like a wimp as we move to forgive someone. We can't always wait until we feel like doing "the right thing" before we do it, because, unfortunately, we don't always feel like doing the right thing. We usually feel like doing the easiest thing.

- Often, confessing our fear to someone defuses it, and courage magically appears. I do this all the time now. When I have to confront someone I need to forgive, I first go to a neutral party and talk about my fear. I think the act of getting it out in the open takes away its power. I can usually exercise the courage to forgive once I've expressed any fear connected to the offense.

Remember how you felt the first time you spoke in public, joined a group where you didn't know anyone, took a new job? Everything is scary the first time we do it. Fear is an uncomfortable emotion, and instead of letting ourselves feel it, we usually repress it as fast as we can. Consequently, we rarely give ourselves an opportunity to grow in courage. If we acknowledge our fear and then appeal to God for courage, he will come through. Then we can say with the psalmist, "I sought the LORD, and he answered me; he delivered me from all my fears" (Psalm 34:4).

Forgiving is truly one of the bravest and most loving things we can do for others. Put the shoe on the other foot for a moment. Wouldn't you cheer for someone if you knew that person was working hard to exercise the courage to forgive you? We all do stupid things, sometimes mean things, things that we need forgiveness for. Don't you want to know when you've hurt someone, when there's something that someone is holding against you? Don't you want to validate the people in your life when you know you've hurt them? Don't you want the opportunity to ask for forgiveness and be forgiven so that everyone can go on?

I do. You're not alone in this. Forgiveness is something we all do for each other in the body of Christ. We're all growing in courage—it's a joint effort. If no one in your circle of influence has started the ball rolling, you be the first.

## Ask Yourself

Where do I need to grow in courage when it comes to forgiveness?

Do I even have a desire to grow in courage? Are there any little steps I can take to exercise courage before I take the big step of forgiving my offender(s)?

What step can I take, in spite of the fear, to exercise courage and forgive my world?

## To Do

Identify whom it is you're afraid to forgive. Take a step toward that person. It may mean taking a deep breath and telling another person "out of the blue" what was hurtful to you. Let yourself feel the courage it took to take that step. Courage can become as addictive as fear.

*Chapter Fifteen*

# grieving
# the pain

"Mom's gone."

My brother's words were real, but I felt like I was in a dream. Gone forever was the hope for the connection I'd always longed for with my mother.

Of course, what I had hoped for was a fantasy. I had wanted a loving, caring relationship with a mother. But, as I should have realized long ago, it could never have been with *this* mother, *my* mother. One thing that had kept me from realizing it was the fact that I had never grieved what I hadn't received from her. I kept longing and expecting her to change—instead of facing reality and accepting her for who she was.

Disconnected from her feelings, Mom was unable to relate on an emotional level with others, leaving me to wonder if she ever really cared about me. I had felt she had abandoned me. My hurt grew to a fury that I never owned until my rage started expressing itself to everyone *but* my mother. Around her, I acted as if everything was fine. When I could no longer contain my anger in her presence, I stayed away, leaving her to wonder what had happened. I was young, immature. I didn't know how to vulnerably confront her so that our relationship could be healed. By the time I realized she was unaware of my hurt, she was gone. Our relationship was over. I was left to grieve.

Not long after receiving my brother's phone call, I started crying. I didn't stop for two months. I cried every day, whenever I wasn't in a meeting at work or with people. What was wrong with me? I soon discovered—nothing. Everything was right. My mother's death opened up all the grief I'd stored inside for who knows how long, probably since I was born. If my heart was to heal, I needed to feel the pain of loss, and so I did all I could to facilitate the grieving process. Big time. I looked at pictures of my mother, listened over and over again to songs that reminded me of her or of our relationship, talked to those who knew her. I knew—finally—that remembering and feeling was part of healing, and I wanted to cooperate.

When we grieve, we acknowledge our pain. We say, "Ouch—this hurts!" To grieve is to admit our humanness, to concede that, yes, we have a heart and, yes, others have the power to break that heart. (Men seem to have more difficulty admitting this than women.)

Unfortunately, some of us grieve only when someone dies. Perhaps we think this is the only time we have the right to feel grief. Or maybe we finally feel safe to let down our guard, knowing others expect us to cry when someone dies. We have preconceived ideas about when it's acceptable to show strong emotions and when it's not. For example, have you ever felt more comfortable hugging someone at the airport than when you see that person on the street? I find this sad. Our ability to get in touch with our deep feelings is too often based on how comfortable or uncomfortable our tears are for those around us.

Whom are we trying to impress? What we sometimes forget is that those who are "real," like the velveteen rabbit in the story of that name, "don't mind being hurt." They know that although "it doesn't often happen to people who break easily, or have sharp edges, or who have to be carefully kept...generally, by the time you are Real, most of your hair has been loved off, and your eyes drop out and you get loose in the joints and very shabby, but...these things don't matter at all, because once you are Real you can't be ugly, except to people who don't understand."[1]

We can let ourselves feel with these folks—the ones who *do* understand. When we do, we model vulnerability and forgiveness. This is what I believe Jesus meant when he told us to share the gospel with others—not just to pronounce that Jesus died on the cross, but to model all that he was when he was alive.

In recent years I've made the choice to be a vulnerable person, committed to staying in touch with and expressing my feelings. Depending on the situation, I may do this alone or with others. I felt I had to make this decision because I realized I was beginning to treat others unkindly. Instead of acknowledging the pain when someone hurt me, I would pretend that I was above being hurt, that I didn't care, and I would go on my merry way. Of course, that never works. As I internalized my pain, my way was becoming less and less merry, and I lashed out at those who got in my way.

What does getting in touch with our feelings and grieving have to do with forgiveness? Everything. Until we acknowledge our pain and express it by grieving, we can't forgive those who hurt us. Until we acknowledge that we are hurt, we won't even know we need to forgive. And until we grieve our hurt, we won't be *able* to forgive. Because I ignored my feelings, I wasn't able to grieve and forgive my mother while she was alive. I believe God has forgiven me for that.

The Roman soldiers didn't ask for forgiveness for their ignorance in putting to death the Son of God, yet Jesus offered it freely. I want to do the same for those who hurt me. I am determined to keep short accounts of the wrongs done to me, to grieve any offenses, to forgive and comfort those who hurt me—to reaffirm my love for them. I am determined not to internalize my pain.

If you want to love your world, I encourage you to join me in this determination.

## Ask Yourself

What do I usually do when feelings of pain or grief surface? Do I even recognize feelings of pain or grief? How often do I let myself cry—no matter how silly or serious the situation?

Do I let others determine whether I will be real and feel my feelings? Can I do the brave thing and let myself feel in front of others?

Have I grieved the relational conflicts in my life, the ones that have caused me serious pain? Have I let myself hurt? Have I stayed with the feelings long enough to be able to interpret their meaning and integrate them into my life?

Can I take a step toward forgiving those connected to my pain?

## To Do

Spend some time today with your feelings. Think through recent hurts and past hurts. In your memories, when you get to some uncomfortable feelings, stop and let them be there. If you feel like crying, do so. It may take some jarring loose of some buried feelings. Sometimes watching a movie can help. (When crying at a sad movie, we are seldom crying over the characters on the screen.) Or try reading a book or engaging in a conversation with a friend. Stay with the feelings long enough to forgive.

1. Margery Williams, *The Velveteen Rabbit* (New York: Simon & Schuster, 1983), 6.

# arriving at compassion

Compassion and forgiveness are intertwined. You can't have one without the other.

If we could practice compassion on a daily basis, forgiveness would cease to be a problem. But how many of us are compassionate when someone who is tired or stressed—whether a coworker, a spouse, or a child—verbally attacks us? How often do we respond in compassion when someone does something to hurt us? Do we even stop to think that the striking out may not have anything to do with us, that the offender is suffering in some way and needs our compassion?

So often we internalize every insult, every offense, every unkind action, or what we perceive as insulting, offensive, or unkind. And when we internalize these things, we go immediately not to compassion but to either anger or self-pity.

When compassion is present, we know we're on our way to

forgiveness, if we're not already there. While we cannot force compassion, we can pray for it, open our heart to it, and receive it. Compassion, like forgiveness, is a gift that God gives so that we can live in the world without anger and judgment.

When we're in the forgiveness process, we move in and out of anger, hurt, betrayal, rage, and grief. If we have asked God to give us a compassionate heart, he will, even in the midst of the process. He will give us a glimpse of compassion—if we're looking. Many people, those who aren't interested in a lifestyle of forgiveness, never do get that glimpse; they don't recognize compassion because they're not looking or longing for it. On the other hand, those who do have compassion aren't "special" in the sense of being "chosen" or uniquely blessed; God gives each of us the same opportunity to grow and develop compassion.

If you "hunger and thirst for righteousness" (Matthew 5:6), you will seek to offer compassion because Jesus did. Part of being a follower of Christ is showing compassion. When we're filled with compassion for others, forgiveness is hardly an issue. I've noticed this as I've gotten older. My growth in compassion has made me more tolerant of differences in others. I don't have to work at forgiveness like I once did because not as much bothers me.

To have compassion for others is to forgive them for their ignorance, to accept them for their seeming lack of interest in spiritual truths, and to love them in all their weirdness and differences. Jesus showed compassion—not only to his disciples, but also to the throngs of people who followed him and with whom he interacted on a daily basis. He offered compassion to the people in his world. Even though he was misunderstood, betrayed, spit upon, ridiculed, and finally crucified, he always came from a place of compassion, not from a place of self-pity or rage.

How can you and I become compassionate? I believe compassion starts with giving up a few things:

- our right to be right
- our assumptions that we know where everyone, especially our offenders, are coming from in their offenses
- our value judgments toward our offenders
- our self-pity and lengthy wound-licking sessions
- our tendency to internalize every offense and the ensuing drama our internalizing unfolds

If we truly want to be loving and forgiving people in our world, we must understand the connection between forgiveness and compassion. Compassion is a gift, but it's also a tool that we can use to get us to a place of forgiveness. When we are able to see that others are suffering and that their pain is the source of their hostility, anger, and personal attacks, we can look at them with compassion. We can detach ourselves from the arrows that would penetrate our souls and spirits—the kinds of arrows that cause wounds so deep we wonder if we'll ever be able to forgive, if we'll ever feel love again.

In a broader sense, I've begun to experience transformation in this area as I've started volunteering at the prison near my home. I haven't asked the men about their crimes, but sometimes as we've gotten to know each other, they've confided in me. I've heard stories of gross injustice, abuse, and craziness that have shaped and molded some of these once-little boys into the kind of grown men who, caught off guard, have lost control and acted more aggressively than even they wanted to. Getting to know these men as individuals has enabled me to feel compassion for them and to forgive them for what they have done. I've learned that the majority of people who attack others don't do so unprovoked—not to say that any provocation justifies violent behavior. Many kinds of mental illnesses and much drug abuse, for instance, originated when someone somewhere abused a little person in some way. This fact alone should lead us to a place of compassion for those who live lifestyles of violence rather than love and forgiveness.

As one who has "been there, done that," I know God can transform a hostile, hardhearted, and bitter person into a more compassionate and forgiving person. No, I haven't done anything that could land me in prison, but that's not because I'm better than the inmates I visit. I have simply had the opportunity to make different choices, and I'm grateful I started making those choices before I did do something that landed me in prison! When we see ourselves as equal with others rather than above them, when we recognize ourselves as recipients of God's compassion and forgiveness, then we can extend that same compassion and forgiveness to others no matter what they've done.

What does it look like to offer compassion to others on a daily basis? I can think of no better picture than the ones Jesus provided when he:

- told Peter to shepherd his flock after Peter had betrayed him (John 21:15-23)
- forgave the very people who crucified him because "they do not know what they are doing" (Luke 23:34)
- confronted the men who accused the woman caught in adultery and then told the woman that he didn't condemn her either (John 8:11)
- forgives us when time after time we blow God's opportunities to love and forgive

We show compassion when we look beyond someone's mean actions and see that person's need. We offer compassion when we pray for our offender and wish him or her well rather than evil. We demonstrate compassion when we choose to respond to an offense with forgiveness rather than react with hateful words and/or thoughts.

You and I are on the receiving end of God's compassion every moment of every day. This alone should bring us to a new awareness that we have what it takes to offer the same compassion to others.

*Ask Yourself*
As I look around me, for whom do I have the most compassion?

For whom do I have the least compassion? Do I have any personal issues that are affecting my ability to feel compassion for these people?

What am I willing to do to take some strides toward closing the gap between others and myself when it comes to compassion and forgiveness?

Is there someone in my life for whom I now have little compassion but to whom I could reach out so that I might grow in both compassion and forgiveness?

*To Do*
Prayerfully look around you and find the individual or group of individuals that brings out zero compassion in you. Perhaps they even bring out feelings of hostility. Be honest. Take a loving step toward them. Take another. When you take the step, compassion often grows. Forgiveness will become less of an issue the more compassion grows.

*Chapter Seventeen*

# integrating the
# process

The healing process goes on and on and on...for as long as we live. In one sense, we are whole because that's the way God made us and views us. In another sense, we are always growing and being healed from hurts and wounds inflicted on us by unsuspecting others.

People don't usually intend to hurt us. The wounds just happen as we're tripping through life. But if we can learn to integrate our wounds as they happen, they won't have a chance to rot and poison our whole spiritual system. To integrate a wound means to accept it rather than reject or deny it, to take it in and feel the pain and then to allow it to become a part of the whole of who we are through the process of forgiveness.

When someone hurts us, we always have a number of choices—to hate, to become bitter, to try to get revenge, to withdraw, to close off, and to repress and/or deny that anything happened. Or we can begin the process of forgiveness. The minute we remember forgiveness, we're beginning to integrate our wound.

How does integration occur?

Practically, integration is the result of the daily forgiveness process that we've been discussing throughout this book. (1) We decide to be a forgiving person. (2) We commit to asking for forgiveness when we've hurt someone. (3) We choose to forgive others when they've hurt us. Sounds simple enough.

It's not.

What too often happens is that we get hurt and immediately blame ourselves and/or view others in a judgmental light. Or we pretend the hurt didn't happen, but deep down we've already internalized it and the wound remains buried, ready to influence and inform our lives in the future whenever a similar experience happens or a similar feeling surfaces.

Let's look at the process of integration step by step:

*1. We decide to be a forgiving person.*

When we decide we're not going to hold on to resentment, bitterness, and hostility toward others, we decide to pay attention to each and every thing that hurts us. No more thinking we're "too sensitive" or "that shouldn't bother me" or "he didn't mean it." These are things we tell ourselves to cover our pain at getting hurt—again. When we're committed to integrating our wounds, it doesn't mean we no longer get hurt. It means we acknowledge the hurt, no matter how minor or major the offense may seem. What does this look like?

- We acknowledge the pain to ourselves, and possibly to the other person, if it feels like the loving thing to do for the relationship or for the bigger purpose of loving our world.

- We grieve the pain for as long as it takes, accepting that we are in process.
- We make a conscious choice to forgive the other person for the offense, whether or not we feel like it or whether or not that person deserves it.
- We ultimately accept the other person for who he or she is, practicing the compassion we learned about in the last chapter.

If we're committed to doing these four things, we're on our way to integrating our wounds.

*2. We ask for forgiveness when we've hurt someone.*

Forgiveness works both ways. And we must remember that asking for forgiveness doesn't mean we've always done something wrong. It could just mean that another person has been hurt, and in order to do his or her own integrating he or she needs an opportunity to forgive us. We can't do anything about what we don't know, of course. We have to depend on others to let us know when they've been hurt, and we know this doesn't always happen. Sometimes, we have to do a little detective work.

Your spouse is giving you one-word answers. Whenever you try to talk to him, he mumbles something incoherent. Finally, he snaps at you for no apparent reason. Now this could have something to do with you, and it might not. Ask. If he tells you he's angry with you or hurt, you can ask his forgiveness. Don't defend the actions or words that hurt him. That gets you nowhere. Just ask for forgiveness. Later, if you want to do some explaining, that's okay. But he first needs validation and the opportunity to forgive you so he can once again be open to what you have to say.

*3. We forgive others when they've hurt us.*

Attitude is important here. We don't always have to tell the other person that we're forgiving him or her. Sometimes saying, "I forgive you," even if you really do, sounds self-righteous and pious. It depends on where the person is. If he or she comes to you and asks for forgiveness, then yes, it's important to offer the gift of forgiveness out loud. But if the other person doesn't even know you feel hurt or if you suspect the person wouldn't care, then you'll only make a fool of yourself by announcing that you forgive him or her. You have to move carefully here. You want to follow what God is telling you to do, but you don't want to make a public issue out of something that is a personal issue. If you say "I forgive you" to some people, they won't even know what you're talking about.

In our closest relationships, loving one another means validating one another's wounds so that we can help each other complete the process of forgiveness. I had a friend who was always saying, "You need to forgive me, just forgive me," whenever I was the one who was hurt. She never admitted that she had hurt me. I *wanted* to forgive her, but in order for us to stay emotionally close, I needed her to validate my pain. She finally got it, and the process suddenly became a lot easier for both of us.

Of course, the deeper the wound, the more complicated the integration process. The important thing is to get started and to commit to the ongoing work.

That's all God expects.

## Ask Yourself

How well do I integrate offenses as they come to me? Am I skipping any of the necessary steps?

Is there anything I can do to remind myself of the steps when I'm in the middle of working through an offense?

Am I in any of the three steps right now? If so, which one and with whom?

## To Do

Consider your most difficult and complicated relationships. If you don't have any difficult and complicated relationships, ask yourself how deeply you're relating to others. All close relationships get difficult and complicated at times. Identify where you are in the integration process in each so that you can take conscious steps toward walking a forgiveness lifestyle.

# Chapter Eighteen

# not again

I sat in the darkened movie theater next to my two friends, munching my popcorn and watching the movie *The Apostle*. I felt as if my life with my ex-husband was being replayed before me on a large screen. *Everyone can change,* I reminded myself. I had spent years actively working through my feelings toward my ex-husband so that I could look on him with compassion and forgiveness.

I was taken completely off guard when, during the movie, I found myself suddenly shaking and sobbing. I was trying not to disturb my friends, but my emotions were uncontrollable. I began sobbing at the point in the movie when "the apostle" was obviously preparing to hit his wife. His rage escalated as the two of them sat together on the couch and talked. I recognized all too well the look of terror on the wife's face, and without warning the memories surfaced.

The scene finally ended, but I'm not sure how it ended. I honestly can't remember if he followed through and hit her or not. I blocked out the rest of the scene. I walked out of the theater wondering, *Haven't I forgiven him? How could all that emotion still be in there? What was that about?*

As I prayed and thought about it, I was reminded of what I'd read about Vietnam vets. Many still suffer aftershocks from the war even though it ended more than twenty-five years ago. Their wartime experiences were so traumatic, they still suffer the effects. Could that be what this was? Posttraumatic stress syndrome? I decided maybe so. But I went through the process of forgiving my ex-husband once again, just in case. I felt the pain of the abuse and reminded myself that he couldn't do any better, because he didn't know any better. Once again I was brought to a place of compassion and finally forgiveness.

Remember, the more deeply we're hurt, the more difficult (and often lengthy) the forgiveness process. It's not helpful to condemn ourselves because we are still in pain. Instead, we can view the resurfacing of old pain as the gift of yet one more opportunity to heal our wounds. The reemergence of "old pain" presents us with another opportunity to practice forgiveness. A lot of the pressure we feel to be "through with forgiveness" comes from the way we think others will perceive us if they know we are still struggling with "that old thing," whatever it is. We're embarrassed that we're not completely through the process. The offense happened years and years ago, and here we are still having feelings about it.

When you've done a lot of work to forgive past hurts, moments like I had in the movie theater can be discouraging. It's difficult to understand why past hurts would resurface when you think you've done all that you need to do to move on. If we're not careful, such feelings can distract us from the work we need to do. The truth is, whether or not we understand them, the feelings are real and therefore need our attention.

We need to go with what *is* rather than what we think should be. We can't and won't always be able to understand our feelings and reactions. We can't always pin down emotional pain and its causes and cures. Rather than listen to those well-meaning folks who tell us we're "being ruled by our emotions," we can ask God for insight when an emotion surfaces, whether it's fear or anger or grief. "What's this about, God? What can I learn from this? If I need to forgive once again, I'm willing to do that. Just show me what you want me to do so that I can continue to grow in your love."

Because I'm afraid I may have a negative reaction or emotion, I sometimes avoid situations. Weddings. Certain kinds of churches. Even social gatherings if specific people are going to be there. I wish it wasn't so. I wish I was above feeling hurt over things that have happened to me. I wish I was so eager to grow and let God transform me, I didn't avoid pain. Sometimes I'm brave, and I head into it. But if I see it coming…well, I try not to be a chicken, but sometimes I am. I want to walk in forgiveness, I just don't always want to go through the pain it takes to get there—one more time.

It helps me to remember that God loves me and is concerned that I am becoming more like Christ, that I am becoming more loving and forgiving. God never promised us that life would be pain-free, and he often uses pain to get our attention. I don't always like it, nor do I understand it, but I also believe that he knows what's best for me. And so I pray that he will help me forgive. Again. And again. And yet again.

I believe that someday I'll watch *The Apostle* again, and when I do, I won't tremble and sob. Because I'll be better. I believe, and you can believe, that we are continuing to heal—because we're choosing to live a life of forgiveness.

*Ask Yourself*

Is there a relationship or experience that continues to haunt me, trail me, even though I've dealt with it many times? Can I look at it just one more time, maybe from a different angle?

How can I learn to be more patient with myself when I have recurring memories that bring up old pain and anger? How might I remind myself that when I feel old pain, it's not because I'm a whiner but because God is offering me another opportunity to heal?

Is it possible that God orchestrates events and situations, brings people into my life who will be my teachers and healers? What might he be telling me through someone who continues to haunt me? Can I listen to him?

*To Do*

Take a look at everything that has ever surfaced pain for you. Rather than shove it aside for a rainy day, take it out and study it. What do you feel? Are you truly free to love yourself the way you are right now? Forgive anyone connected to your pain. Again. And again. And yet again. Forgive as often as it takes to free you.

# Chapter Nineteen

# when forgiveness is undeserved

Exactly one year ago my single friend Diane moved in with her eighty-one-year-old mother to help her out as she made the transition from her large home to a retirement apartment. At first they seemed quite happy living together, cooking for one another, sharing stories in the evenings, enjoying each other's company.

But somewhere along the line, things took a nasty turn. Diane's mother began to use a certain angry tone with her daughter that Diane began to resent. Of course, a "tone" in our voice isn't there without a reason. It's the result of a feeling we're unable, for whatever reason, to express.

Bewildered, Diane tried to figure out what was happening. Why was her mother treating her so poorly? She didn't treat her other children that way. Of course, Diane's sisters were her mother's "real" children; Diane was a stepchild. Could that be it? Her father had married Diane's stepmother shortly after Diane's mother had died. She had never felt loved by her stepmother. Finally, as the situation worsened, Diane decided it was time to move out, and she told her mother so.

"Well, I hope you have enough money to move out," her mother challenged. Then she added, "Anyway, I only took you in because you were Bill's daughter."

Diane tried to stifle a gasp. Her stepmother thought that *she* was doing *Diane* a favor instead of the other way around! But even more significant, Diane knew that deep down, even if her stepmother was not conscious of it, she was referring to the *first* time she took Diane in, fifty years earlier. Diane had been right all along. This woman had never loved her. All along, their relationship had been not about love but about duty.

Diane got up and walked out of the room, knowing their relationship would never be the same. Now, only a few weeks later, in spite of the tangible tension in their relationship, Diane is committed to forgiving her stepmom. Diane knows her stepmother will likely never apologize because she spoke the truth: the way she had felt about Diane all these years. I don't know if I could do it—be willing to offer forgiveness so quickly. But Diane knows that for now this is her spiritual work, to learn to offer compassion and forgiveness even when it is undeserved.

Diane's "mother" seems oblivious to the deep pain her words and true feelings have caused her "daughter." This may be the most difficult part of our commitment to forgive—the choice to let someone off the hook when it seems that person couldn't care less about our feelings, our lives, the wound they have given us. How is it possible for us to receive a wound and then turn around and offer the other cheek to the person who hurt us, as Jesus told his disciples to do in Matthew 5:39?

Not that Jesus meant we should allow the injustice to go unchallenged. We have only to look at his example to see this. When the high priest was questioning him on the night of Peter's betrayal, one of the officials slapped Jesus because the official didn't like the way Jesus answered a question. In response our Lord said, "If I said something wrong,...testify as to what is wrong. But if I spoke the truth, why did you strike me?" (John 18:23).

When Jesus told his disciples to turn the other cheek, he meant that they were not to take revenge. He didn't mean that we should go around letting others abuse us; he meant that we should forgive them and continue to be vulnerable and honest in our relationships. In other words, we don't go off to lick our wounds (well, not for long at least). We must force ourselves to stay in the trenches, to fight and win the battles that come our way. Sometimes that means confronting and dealing with the unpleasant memories of those who have hurt us and who are now merrily living their lives— sometimes still by our sides, oblivious and seemingly uncaring about how they have wounded us.

Recently a friend told me, "I've stopped reading self-help books because I don't want to dig around in that old stuff anymore. I just want to be happy."

I felt sad as I heard these words. Yes, my friend had a point. We don't need to constantly "dig around" in "old stuff." But we do need to keep growing. Maybe growing does require some digging once in a while, but I don't consider myself a digger. I consider myself a warrior. A searcher. A fighter.

It's difficult when those around us aren't aware that there is a battle going on. Especially when our loved ones, the ones who are supposed to be on our side in the trenches, suddenly turn on us and make us the target of their weapons. What a horrific shock! Yet we still have to see these people every day, live with them, commune with them. The enemy is truly in our midst.

If we don't learn to walk in forgiveness and turn the other cheek, we will either live a life of denial in our relationships or we will tear down and wound each other in an effort to cover up our true feelings, which we believe to be unacceptable. For example, if Diane's mother could simply share her heart, even if the facts are painful—if she could just say to Diane, "You know, when I married your dad I already had three kids and I was just so overwhelmed with two more, I couldn't cope. I'm so sorry…" If she could just be *honest.* But that will probably never happen, and so she will continue to tear Diane down in order to avoid her true feelings—feelings that are too painful to face. Consequently, Diane will be left to walk the road of forgiveness alone. Over and over and over again.

A few years ago there was a woman in the news who shot and killed her son's molester in the courtroom during the trial. I wonder. Had she tried first to forgive? Maybe. Maybe she tried, and maybe she just couldn't find it in herself to give. But she did have a choice. We all have a choice—to pick up a weapon or offer a gift.

Forgiveness is always a choice. No one can make us forgive or not forgive. Therein lies its power. When forgiveness—rather than vengeance—is our focus, we are protected from the deep gashes and wounds that others would inflict upon us. We may feel the sting or the searing pain of a deep gash, but we don't go down. When we're choosing to walk in forgiveness—not because we want to do the right thing or even because the Bible says we should, but because we want to be more like Jesus and love our world—we can. We can transcend our circumstances.

*Ask Yourself*

Is there anyone in my life I know I need to forgive but whom I believe to be undeserving? What do I believe to be my role in this person's or these persons' lives?

How can I have compassion for spiteful, mean, uncaring people, especially when they are the ones closest in my life?

How can I take the high road when everything in me wants to run for cover? How can I love those who can't or won't see that their words and actions are causing me pain? What is God calling me to?

*To Do*

Think of a creative way this week to approach that person who does not deserve your forgiveness. Without letting this person off the hook, how can you respond in love to accusations, indirect comments, hurtful remarks? How can you maintain your own self-respect and dignity and at the same time walk in forgiveness and compassion toward this person?

# Chapter Twenty

# first lovers,
# then forgivers

I made the choice to love my world before I knew that such a choice also meant forgiving the people in my world. Once I realized that, I had to rethink my commitment to love. I'm beginning to understand that loving one's world means a lot of things: extending grace and mercy when it's not deserved, being gentle when you want to beat somebody up, exercising patience when you feel you have none. Forgiveness is just one item on a long list of gifts we give to others when we decide to love.

When we forgive, we make evident our decision to love our world. We couldn't forgive if we didn't love first. Don't those Christlike people who forgive the most horrific crimes imaginable against them and their loved ones amaze you? It takes supernatural strength to forgive your child's killer or the man who raped you or the parent who beat you. How is it possible to extend compassion and forgiveness to these people?

In recent years I've heard it said that it is a mistake for victims to forgive their abusers. Those who take this position claim that moving quickly toward forgiveness short-circuits the healing process that is necessary for wholeness. While it's true that each situation is different, we need to listen carefully to God's voice in our hearts on this. But too often, rather than listen to God, we listen to the collective voices of the therapists or family members or friends.

Everyone has an opinion about what we need to do. Pretty soon we can't hear our own voice *or* God's voice—the two voices that speak the most quietly and the two voices that hold the most truth. Sadly, we sometimes block out these voices because we don't trust them. Yet loving—forgiving—our world is only possible when we are able to sort out God's voice from the clamor and then listen to our own heart as it responds to what God is saying. Only then will we have the tools to love our world.

Just this week a friend called and wanted to see me. She hadn't contacted me for more than three years. Our last correspondence had been a phone call in which she had promised to meet me at a conference that weekend. We'd made plans to spend the day before the conference together. She never showed up, and she never called to apologize or tell me what happened. We hadn't spoken again until the other day.

This friend wasn't a casual friend. We'd known each other for nine years. We'd shared intimate secrets, cried together, laughed together—you know, everything it takes to bond two people. And then suddenly, just like that, she was gone.

I missed her.

But she'd obviously for some reason decided she didn't want me in her life. That was her choice. I had been bewildered. Angry.

Hurt. Now here she was, in my face, just as suddenly as she'd disappeared three years before.

We met at a restaurant. "I was depressed," she told me. "I didn't know it. I couldn't fight anymore. I was suicidal… I knew you'd hold me accountable. You ask too many questions… My marriage… It had nothing to do with you. I just couldn't…" She went on, and while I cared tremendously about everything she was telling me, I knew the facts of her disappearance were irrelevant to my task at the moment. The title of a Smokey Robinson song flashed before me (God will use whatever you let him.): "Love Don't Give No Reason." I didn't need to hear her story in order to extend love to my friend, in order to forgive her. I didn't need a reason to love her. When it comes to things like love and forgiveness, I'm finding that the reasons don't matter a whole lot. What matters is a heart turned away from self-protection and fear and turned toward loving God, others, and ourselves.

God has one expectation of us—that everything we do in the world, all that we are—be an expression of the two greatest commandments: "Love the Lord your God with all your heart and with all your soul and with all your mind and with all your strength" and "Love your neighbor as yourself" (Mark 12:30-31).

This scripture tells us *what* we are to do. Another scripture tells us *how:* "Be kind and compassionate to one another, forgiving each other, just as in Christ God forgave you. Be imitators of God, therefore, as dearly loved children and live a life of love, just as Christ loved us and gave himself up for us" (Ephesians 4:32–5:2). It's no accident that these last two verses—one about forgiveness and one about love—are linked together. We cannot have one without the other.

"I'm angry," I told my friend now. "Hurt. I don't understand everything you're telling me."

She nodded.

"But I know I need to forgive you. No, I *want* to forgive you."

"Can you? I really am so sorry."

"Yes, I can. Of course I can." And as I said the words, I knew they were true. "I do—forgive you."

You see, I'd already made the decision to love my world. How could I *not* forgive my friend when I already loved her? At one time, she had been a central part of my life, held a central place in my heart. I wanted to open that place back up to her, and the only way I could do that was to reach out with God's compassion and forgive her. To give up the hurt and recover the love.

I'm able to move more quickly to forgiveness than I used to. I'm more aware of the way I feel toward someone and my need to forgive him or her. I don't have to think about it as long. I don't have to lick my wounds in public. I don't even have to punish the offender by withholding my love and forgiveness in order to make that person suffer. For me, forgiveness is not an *if* but a *when.* Not *what* but *how.* That's what happens when we allow God to change our hearts and to cause us to grow.

The results of making the choice to forgive are far-reaching. Forgiveness makes us better people. The decision to become a forgiver teaches us:

1. Vulnerability: We are forced to admit our hurt so that we can forgive our offender.

2. Openness: When we learn to extend forgiveness, we can also learn to ask for and receive it from others.

3. Courage: We can move toward others in love, knowing they

have no power to hurt us unless we allow it. If we do allow it, all is not lost, as we have learned an even greater power—that of forgiveness.

Forgiveness is a walk, a journey that we decide to take. Like any journey, it starts with one step: the decision to love.

*Ask Yourself*

Am I able to see the connection between loving and forgiving my world in my relationships with friends and family?

Can I see how loving and forgiving relate to each other in my relationships with my enemies? Is there anyone I'm willing to love but not to forgive?

How can I close the gap between the two and make it one act, integrate both gifts into my life and so into all my relationships?

Where am I in the process of and commitment to loving and forgiving my world?

*To Do*

Think about one person you've been willing to love but unwilling to forgive. Can you go a step further and forgive what doesn't seem forgivable? How can you express that forgiveness in a tangible way?

# Chapter Twenty-One

# the vow

What about it? Do you want to grow in forgiveness? Would you like to be a forgiver? Have you changed as you've read this book and explored your feelings? How? Do you want to keep changing?

When we first make the commitment to love or to forgive or to walk in compassion toward others, we don't know all that will be required of us. I remember thinking, *Oh sure, forgiveness, that's part of being a Christian. The Bible makes that pretty clear. No big deal, everyone makes mistakes, we all need forgiveness from time to time, no problem...*

But then life's injustices got in the way. I began to resist feeling the pain of those injustices, maybe because somewhere deep down I knew that if I let myself feel them, I'd be required to forgive. When I first signed up to be a follower of Christ and a lover of my world, I hadn't known the kinds of things I would be asked to forgive.

At first, forgiving those who'd offended me seemed too much to ask. But then I considered the alternative, and that was scarier still. Did I want to be a bitter old person, hating everyone, thinking everyone was out to get me? Did I want to be closed off to the world and to love, calling myself a Christian but refusing to walk in the principles I said I believed in? Did I want to be a hypocrite?

Forgiveness is not a new idea. You've certainly read magazine articles and books on the subject many times over. It's even become a mainstream idea, discussed at length on talk shows and news shows. Many people are recognizing the power of forgiveness and even the physical damage an unforgiving heart can do to the body. The *Seattle Times* ran an article recently on the benefits of forgiveness:

> A 1998 Stanford study of young adults who had felt hurt or offended showed forgiveness could substantially reduce the amount of anger they harbored. Anger has been associated with an increased risk of heart attacks and it negatively influences the body's immune system.
>
> The notion that anger and an unwillingness to forgive can damage the physique as well as the psyche has gotten a boost from new research from the University of Wisconsin in Madison. Investigators there, who have not yet published their findings, have found that the less people forgave, the more diseases they had and the more medical symptoms they reported.
>
> "We've been surprised at how strong forgiveness can be as a healing agent for people," says Robert Enright, professor of educational psychology at the university who in 1985 created the country's first

forgiveness research program. "You can actually
change a person's well-being, their emotions, by
helping them to forgive.[1]

There's no argument about the benefits of forgiveness. There's
no question that forgiveness can only be good for you and your
relationships. There's no doubt as to what God wants for you.

The decision is yours: Do you want to do the work it takes to
make forgiveness a lifestyle?

Making a commitment is one thing; making a vow is another.
If forgiveness is something you want God to work into you, into
the very fiber of your being, then I suggest you make a vow to
become not only a lover but also a forgiver in the world in which
you find yourself every day. I suggest you pray the following prayer:

I choose to forgive others for any offenses done to me
in the past and in the present and for any offenses
that may be committed against me in the future. I
choose to make forgiveness a way of life, no matter
whom it is I'm called upon to forgive or how heinous
the offense might be. And I choose to ask for forgiveness whenever I wrong anyone else so that others,
too, might be given the opportunity to be free.

Congratulations. You have just embarked on one of the most
satisfying and life-changing journeys you'll ever take—both for you
and for those whom your life touches. Can you hear God's
applause?

1. Julie Sevrens, "Forgiveness? It Just Might Enhance Physical Health, Too," *Seattle
Times,* 4 July 1999.

If you enjoyed this book by
Gloria Chisholm, look for the companion book,
*Love One Another* (1-57856-310-0),
available at your local Christian bookstore.

PERSONAL NOTES